Kafka in China

Part One

♦ The People's Republic of Corruption ♦

A Personal Memoir

Warren Henry Rothman

dedication

This book is dedicated to the astoundingly brave Chinese citizens and legal professionals who fight for Rule of Law, human rights, and transparency in government, in the face of torture, imprisonment, and murder by a kleptocratic Chinese Communist tyranny that must silence them in order to preserve its monopoly on power and ensure that the Communist Party's leaders and their cronies keep the fruits of their plunder.

Thank you for your interest in **KAFKA IN CHINA, Part One.** As a
SPECIAL FREE OFFER get a current copy of my newsletter,
CHINA REALIST, on Chinese politics and human rights and
international relations (a $5.99 value) by signing up via this link:
kafkainchina.com/newsletter-offer-1

Warren Henry Rothman

acknowledgments

Friendship is the force that brought me through the trauma that I suffered in China in October 2008, the friendship of many people, some who knew what I had been through, some who did not. To friendship I also owe this book. While I am solely responsible for the accuracy of the facts and for the conclusions and theories set forth herein, my friends urged me to write my story and graciously and generously commented on numerous drafts, improving them as much as possible. For their patient and helpful criticism and encouragement throughout, I could never thank enough: Professor R. Howard Bloch, J. Kirk Casselman, Esq., M. Ignatius Cronin, Robert E. Hammond, M.D., Frederick C. Kneip, Esq., Professor Williamson Murray, Kenneth W. Orce, Esq., Jeffrey J. Parish, Esq., David L. Roscoe III, Professor Rosalind Rosenberg, John M. Shank, Michael C. Shealy, Professor M. Lewis Spratlan, and Chilton Thomson, Jr. I am very grateful to Louise Casselman for designing this book.

Cover by Louise Casselman

Photographs by Warren Henry Rothman

prologue

When I saw the first reports of the Neil Heywood case in February 2012, I was dumbfounded that a Westerner had been murdered in China. I had never heard of more than a handful of foreigners even being seriously harmed there. Heywood allegedly had been laundering money for the family of a top Chinese official. My case also involved high-level corruption, although my sole involvement was to be the unfortunate audience of a blurt-out about a bribe. Heywood almost disappeared without a trace, and I came very close to such an end in October 2008. As the facts came out about the Heywood murder, even more chilling parallels emerged.

Something in the initial reports about the murder made me look in a batch of papers dating from my ordeal that I had tossed in a file cabinet on my return to the US in November 2008 and had never read. It was then that I discovered the letters on the letterhead of the US Consulate General in Shanghai that are reproduced on pages xii and xiii. The letters solved a few questions but added new ones, the most shocking of all. Is it possible that a US consulate, without so much as having interviewed me or contacted my family, delivered me to the hell of a Chinese mental hospital? If so, on what basis and by what authority? Or, had the individuals behind it all run the tremendous risk of forging the letters? Strenuous efforts by me and on my behalf to find the answers to these questions have been met with a stone wall.

It also was in 2012 that a series of unprecedentedly detailed and numerous reports spewed forth about rampant Chinese human rights abuses, including the use of fraudulent incarceration in mental hospitals, imprisonment in black jails and labor camps, and covert murders to silence people, political dissidents, members of unapproved religious groups, inconvenient relatives, peasant petitioners trying to get back illegally confiscated land. But no one I have spoken to has ever heard of another Westerner being thrown into a Chinese mental hospital. For several years, I had been telling friends about what happened to me, but once the Heywood murder and these human rights abuses became known, I decided to go public with my case. I contacted Joel Brinkley, the eminent journalist, who published two in-depth reports in 2012, in *Politico* and in the *San Francisco Chronicle*, respectively. Now, I have decided to tell my story in full.

I thought hard about the title to this book once it occurred to me. Upon finishing an early draft, I stopped work to read some literary criticism of Kafka to find out whether my reference to him was justified on more than the most obvious metaphorical levels. Then I began to delve into his works for the sheer fascination of it, and the more I read, the more I felt that I had to read everything he wrote, the works I had read years before, the many I had never read.

In the year that I spent reading Kafka, the most unexpected resonance with my story that I found is in his final work, the exquisite and haunting *Josephine the Singer, or the Mouse Folk*. A self-declared "unmusical" man, on his deathbed, unable to speak because of tuberculosis that had spread to his larynx, Kafka celebrates singing as a supremely powerful social force and source of solace:

> Our singer is called Josephine. Anyone who has not heard her does not know the power of song.

...if her singing does not drive away the evil, at least it gives us the strength to bear it.

This at least is the view of Josephine's supporters. I count myself among them. Music and singing have been at the center of my life since earliest childhood, my deepest sources of enjoyment and self-expression. In October 2008 and afterward, they became as well indispensable agents of healing in the face of monstrous evil, possibly even life-saving defenses.

Warren Henry Rothman

CONSULATE GENERAL OF THE
UNITED STATES OF AMERICA
Shanghai, China

October 23, 2008

To Whom it May Concern:

We understand that Mr. Warren Rothman, a US Citizen holding US Passport Number ████████ is in need of urgent medical and psychiatric attention. Until we can arrange further details regarding his return to the United States, we understand Mr. ████ [Q.] (08OCT2008, Male, 身份证号码: ████████████) has an ongoing friendship with Mr. Rothman, and is best capable to see to his immediate needs at this time, including hospital admittance and related procedures.

████████████
Acting Consular Chief
US Consulate General in Shanghai

CONSULATE GENERAL OF THE
UNITED STATES OF AMERICA

Oct. 23, 2008

The U. S. Consulate General in Shanghai confirms that Warren Henry Rothman is a U. S. Citizen holding passport number ▓▓▓▓▓▓▓. We understand that Mr. Rothman appears to be in need of psychiatric and medical care before he can return to the United States. The Consulate General cannot assume responsibility for the cost of any medical care but will work with his family and the Department of State to secure financial assistance.

美国驻上海总领事馆证实 Warren Henry Rothman 系美国公民，持美国护照号 ▓▓▓▓▓▓▓。他急需接受心理及药物治疗。美国领馆公民服务处不负担他的治疗费用，但会与其家属联系由其家属支付医疗费用。

在此感谢贵院的帮助。

Consular Section
American Consulate General
Shanghai, China

chapter one

I awoke to discover that a mechanical elastic sleeve was massaging my left forearm and wrist.

"So that's how they hide the wounds of torture victims," I said to myself.

I was in a hospital bed, both forearms tied to the sides, not especially tightly, but such that I could not bring my hands together. They were numb anyway, as if made out of wood.

A masked figure in a nurse's uniform, hair an unnatural orange-red, approached holding a syringe: *Zheli shi yiyuan. Wo shi hushi* [This is a hospital. I am a nurse].[1]

As she positioned my right arm with her left hand, I noticed two black Xs on the paper-thin, cotton pajama top, just below my right shoulder. Usually averse to needles, I didn't feel the shot as it went in. The nurse turned away and came back with another syringe. Now the thought was fully formed: "They are executing me. First the tranquilizer, then the lethal agent."

---

1 English and Mandarin Chinese words and dialogue are expressed as follows:
Italics indicate Mandarin Chinese rendered in pinyin, the Mainland China method of transliterating Mandarin into Roman letters [English translations are in brackets].
["Brackets with English in quotation marks"] are translations of Mandarin where no *pinyin* is supplied.
"Simple quotation marks" indicate speech and thoughts in English.

I tried to yell, but all I could muster was a croak: *Buyao da, buyao da* [Don't inject, don't inject]!

Jiushi rang ni geng piaoliang [It's just to make you more attractive], she replied in a tone so soothing as to be menacing.

A second, mousy-looking nurse entered, interrupting the procedure. She removed the elastic sleeve and asked me some questions. I was so tired and my throat so parched that I could scarcely speak, but I had to try. It seemed that I had a chance to explain myself.

["Then you were not the aggressor?"]

["No, no. I was trying to go out for soup, they grabbed me, threw me back inside."]

["Then, who are your enemies in Shanghai?"]

["Enemies? What enemies? I don't have any enemies in Shanghai."]

From the expression on her face, it seemed to me that the second nurse was considering seriously what I said and that she might even take my side with whomever was in charge of this situation. But no sooner did she leave than the first one came back wielding her syringe.

I felt a surge of that strange, inner-generated current of electricity that I had been experiencing lately. With my last iota of strength, ignoring a sudden, searing pain that shot through the numbness, I ripped my left hand free of its binding to shield my right arm from the needle. The nurse stepped back, seemingly unsure of what to do next. Behind me, I heard a sharp, commanding voice: *Zaoshang sidian, gei ta dazhen* [Give him the shot at 4am], then a muffled conversation and footsteps receding in the distance.

I collapsed on my back, panting, unable to move. A short, slender man darted out from a darkened corner of the room. He smiled ambiguously at me as he tied my hands much more tightly than before to the sides of the bed, clucking his tongue disapprovingly all the while. I asked him for water, but he ignored me, turned out the overhead light, and withdrew to the corner of the room from which he had emerged.

As my eyes became accustomed to the near pitch blackness, I could make out a bed and a form on top buried under blankets. I tried to call out:

Xiansheng, wo kesile. Shui. Qing gei wo shui [Mister, I'm dying of thirst. Water. Please give me water].

No response.

Ni shi shei [Who are you]?

No response.

Now, it hurt to speak, and I gave up trying. I had only a few hours of sleep during the previous 20 days, exhaustion was overtaking fear and pain and thirst, the shot was lulling me into somnolence. But I realized that sleep was the path of least resistance, the one these people expected me to fall into. I resolved to stay awake. I refused to let them murder me without a struggle.

Over and over in my brain: *Geng piaoliang, zaoshang sidian* [More attractive, 4am]. I thought, "'More attractive', as in peacefully dead."

I tried desperately to focus my thinking. I had no idea where I was or who these people were. Enemies? The nurse's question took me aback. I wasn't accustomed to thinking that I had enemies in China. But I wasn't about to tell them that there were at least two. For me the question was, who was the enemy behind the enemies who landed me in this place. "The landlady? Is that possible? Was it just the money?"

I could hear myself start to snore. I was nearly asleep, and the feeling was delicious, irresistible. The sudden memory of a note on a slip of paper that had been left for me to find jolted me into stark consciousness:

3

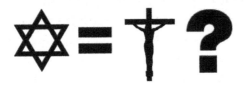

Those symbols, their gruesome threat, sent waves of terror through me that made me wish that I had fallen asleep.

Qiu ni...shui [I beg you... water], I gasped until the sound was reduced to a sigh, audible only to me.

The man in the other bed was so quiet and motionless that he might as well have been dead.

As I lay there, voiceless, I became aware that I could not hear a single sound. The room seemed like a vacuum in outer space.

chapter two

In 1979, Deng Xiaoping instituted his policy of *kaifa kaifang* [developing and opening up], a key aspect of which was to attract foreign trade and investment, and that led to my first trip to China. In February 1980, an unexpected call in my office on Wall Street, just as I was finalizing an SEC filing:

"This is Peter --, I am general counsel of (a Fortune 500 company in San Francisco). I have two questions for you: One. Can you still sing?"

"What the Hell? Some kind of nut," was my first thought. "Yes, Peter, but can I call you later? I have an S-1 amendment at the SEC, and the window is about to go down."

Peter was not put off easily. "Second question: How is your Mandarin, and do you want to go to China? We are negotiating a joint venture there."

"I'll call you back in twenty minutes," I answered.

Peter was an indefatigable networker, and through his battery of Rolodexes he had found me, one of a handful of lawyers then who had studied Chinese language. A lifelong Yalie and an avid Yale singer, Peter was additionally keen to recruit me because he had learned that I had been a Whiffenpoof and a Yale Glee Club soloist. A perfect fit from his standpoint.

China was my great intellectual passion, kindled and fueled by wonderful professors, chief among them Arthur Frederick Wright and Mary Clabaugh Wright, husband and wife, who taught, respectively, pre-Qing Dynasty history (from antiquity until 1644) and Qing Dynasty to the Communist takeover (1644-1949). For nine years, starting Freshman Year, when I needed a personal interview with Mary Wright to take her undergraduate course, otherwise open only to juniors and seniors, through graduate school and law school, I spent a large portion, often the majority, of my time studying some aspect of China, language, archeology, art, and law, in addition to history. Yale had attracted the Wrights from Stanford University, and a fabulous catch they were. Arthur was awarded a prestigious chair in the history department, and Mary joined the department as Yale's first tenured woman professor.

The students called such teachers "spellbinders". The Wrights had very different teaching personalities, but they had many things in common, the magic and passion with which they infused their lectures, their brilliance as scholars, their fierce intellectual honesty, the elegance and clarity of their writing styles. The students hung on their every turn of phrase, drank in their every theory. Above all, the Wrights encouraged students who exhibited critical thinking and who were not afraid to challenge them on their own views, even their published positions. No one who took their courses ever forgot the experience, and in my case, their imprint was indelible and life-changing.

My fate was more or less sealed when on the last day to register for courses before Junior Year I happened to meet Mary Wright on the steps of Sterling Library. She invited me to join her graduate school seminar. That year and Senior Year for my honors thesis with her as my adviser, for the first time in all my schooling I was challenged to my limit, researching and writing on aspects of Qing Dynasty and Republic history, the sheer force of her intellect driving me into realms of thinking that I had never entered before. She never told me what subjects to research or what to think, but with her searching questions she urged me to think, and think, and think some more. One of my fondest memories was her promotion to full professor, news of which leaked out on a Wednesday, the day we convened in her office for the seminar. The four of us stood and applauded as she entered. She smiled with surprise and a certain shyness, her face radiance itself, though not wasting a minute she turned to the subject of the day. It was a tremendous milestone in many ways. I was bewitched by Mary Wright, and that is as true today as it was then.

There were only seven or eight graduate students in Chinese history, not counting me, but they still had factions. As an undergraduate, I had only one semester with Arthur Wright, so I naturally fell into the "Mary camp". But when I was in graduate school, I took a wonderful seminar with him. Then, I understood the ardor of the "Arthur camp" and came to view the Wrights as highly complementary in style as well as subject matter. His profound knowledge and wisdom on classical Chinese philosophy and institutions, his magisterial manner, his fabulous sense of humor, his anecdotes that displayed his greatness as a raconteur, these qualities made him a stupendous and beloved teacher.

Decades after both Wrights had passed away, I ran into a Stanford graduate in Beijing who missed studying with the Wrights because Yale had just grabbed them up. His jaw dropped when I answered his question as to whether I had studied with them when I was at Yale. After a moment he said:

"What an honor!"

I was amazed to meet anyone then who knew the Wrights because both had passed away so long ago. To meet such a person in Beijing, where they lived from June 1941 to September 1943 and for several years after the war, was doubly amazing.

I responded: "I always thought so, but why do you say so?"

A torrent of enthusiasm poured forth from him: "Because they were such brilliant thinkers, such great writers, wonderful lecturers, so meticulous. And they stood up to the McCarthy-ites. Stanford mourned their departure."

In the 1960s, there was little practical use for China studies other than in espionage and academia. There was little question of the former career as I had none of the attributes one normally associates with spies. But academia was a serious possibility and might have been a certainty. I was tremendously inspired by the Wrights, and by their protégé, Jonathan Spence, then a newly minted Ph. D. and already a brilliant star in the Chinese history firmament, and I came very close to agreeing to Mary Wright's urgings that I also pursue a Ph. D.

However, since childhood, I had thought of myself as a singer and loved music more than anything else. When I discovered opera in high school, I set myself the goal of becoming an operatic tenor. In college, my singing voice was just maturing, and I began to study vocal technique. Several voice teachers encouraged my operatic aspirations. The Yale Glee Club summer tour in Europe between Sophomore and Junior Years provided a new level of support. My solo, a German folk song, received particular mention in Dutch and German newspaper reviews of our concerts. After we sang for Nadia Boulanger at her academy in Fontainebleau, that celebrated composer, conductor, and teacher gave me serious encouragement. I met musical figures in Germany who expressed similar views. There I was, in Europe, in the heart and soul of opera. Yet, no matter how glittering the possibilities of a career, they still were only possibilities. All of that happened only weeks before my chance meeting at Sterling Library with Mary Wright.

All through Junior and Senior Years, it became a terrible struggle for me to choose between singing and China. I was just able to balance the two as an undergraduate, but to go any further with either I would have to choose. Each was all-consuming. The all-out academic route required not only Chinese but also Japanese language fluency. At the same time, my voice teacher told me that already I was years behind my peers in vocal technique and musicianship; in addition, I had no stage experience. By the time I could finish a Ph. D., I would be at least 26 or 27 with no time to study voice at all in the interim. Especially not in light of Mary Wright's furious reaction when a certain student told her that he had heard that I was interested in pursuing opera. So the age factor was decisive in my choice then of opera over academia, but since I wanted to keep the latter door open, I applied for a teaching fellowship and went for an M.A.

To complicate matters further, my parents wanted me to go to law school, and they pressured me relentlessly throughout Senior Year. To keep them happy and me on the family dole, I did that as well. It was hardly a satisfactory arrangement, but at least an M.A. was fairly undemanding, and I loved teaching my two sections of European history. Yale Law School was laissez-faire itself, you took it as seriously as you liked, and I took it as little so as possible. One of my roommates was as consumed with D. C. politics as I was with opera, and he spent about 95% of his time working on the staff of a prominent senator. So, during the five years after college, I was in law school and graduate school, but most of all studied in New York City with a "famous voice teacher" and a "famous vocal coach", both connected to the Metropolitan Opera.

In June 1970, I finished my academic degrees. It was a tumultuous and troubling time in the nation, at Yale, and in New Haven. For me personally, the worst was the sudden, grave illness and imminent passing of Mary Wright which caught me completely by surprise and left me tormented with loss and guilt.

And, my singing was at an impasse. My vocal range had contracted rather than expanded despite the best efforts of my teachers. I was now 26, but I was not ready to give up on opera. Through personal references, a few months before graduation I had sought the opinions of two former Metropolitan Opera stars, Martial Singher and Robert Weede. Both were encouraging and generous with advice in their assessments of my voice and in their willingness to teach me. Both noted that I was getting long in the tooth for not being further advanced, but neither thought that it was too late to work toward an international career. Maestro Singher was a great interpreter and musician, but in the end I decided to study with Maestro Weede. He too was an electrifying presence on the stage, having played opposite the legendary Maria Callas numerous times, and most importantly he had an exceptionally brilliant vocal placement which was what I most needed to emulate and learn.

After a long-planned travel adventure over the summer, I moved to San Francisco in order to be near Maestro Weede's ranch in Concord, across the bay, where he lived and taught. A warm-hearted artist and teacher, he did improve my vocal technique in the short time that I got to study with him. He was a baritone, but he easily sang most notes in the tenor range, and his high B flat was enough to make many a tenor weep, not to mention the fact that he liked to demonstrate technique while sitting down, with a lighted cigarette balanced on a tiny ashtray on the top of his huge, bald head, to show that one can sing in any part of the voice with total bodily stillness. I was stricken by the loss of him when he suddenly became ill and died.

At that point, I lost impetus and direction. Within two years, the most important mentors I had ever had were gone, Maestro Weede at 69, Mary Wright far younger, at 52. I did not feel remotely confident about stepping out on an opera stage, and after Mrs. Wright's death, I no longer entertained the idea of academia since I had worked so intensively and personally under her guidance and in her area of Chinese history. So, I moved to New York City to work in the corporate and securities department of the Wall Street law firm where I had clerked during law school summers. I liked and respected tremendously the lawyers there and ultimately formed lifelong friendships, but law was third in interest to me, after opera and China. And in those days in Wall Street law firms, you didn't breathe a word about any interest that competed with the law. You were supposed to be "married to the law," and indeed the crushing work schedule precluded sleep, much less opera singing. After more than six years of it, I felt stifled.

Until Peter's phone call, I had not known that there was work for American lawyers in connection with China. Notwithstanding Nixon's famous 1972 visit, we did not establish diplomatic relations until 1979, and China had scarcely begun to open up. Suddenly, Peter appeared with an offer to head up his company's legal work in China, the rest of Asia, Latin America, and Eastern Europe; travel to these places and opportunities to use my Spanish and French as well as Chinese; encouragement to pursue singing in my spare time; a nice raise, a signing bonus, and San Francisco. As one of the law firm's partners put it, "You hit the Mother Lode!"

I already knew that I loved San Francisco. Fredric, my partner then, now my spouse, wanted to change jobs anyway. It took us no time to decide. We did not want to leave our friends or our flat in a West Village Federal brownstone, but we looked forward to exciting adventures and a place at the top of Telegraph Hill, with 270 degree views of San Francisco Bay.

chapter three

In June 1980, I made my first trip to China. Mao Zedong had been dead for four years, but his memory and legacy both dominated and haunted China. The Great Proletarian Cultural Revolution which Mao launched in May 1966 to demonize and destroy his political rivals and, along with them, traditional Chinese culture, had ended formally with Mao's death in September 1976, but it still was in its last stages. Mao's third and last wife, Jiang Qing, the most hated woman in Chinese history, and the rest of her Gang of Four[2] had been arrested but not yet brought to trial. Hua Guofeng, Mao's personally designated successor, still was in office if no longer in power. In Tiananmen Square, where only a few years before frenzied millions of Red Guards waved copies of Mao's *Little Red Book* and swore eternal fealty to Mao, four huge placards on stilts, of Marx, Engels, Lenin, and Stalin, still faced the famous portrait of Mao over Tiananmen, the Gate of Heavenly Peace. The countryside, including agricultural areas within cities, still was organized into communes, production brigades, and production teams.[3] My company was considering setting up a light industry joint venture with a commune in Shanghai, and a visit to the commune was a trip to the previous century.

China was one gigantic Forbidden City then, a black hole, poorer and more backward and cut off from the rest of the world than North Korea is today. Westerners "went in" to China and mostly weren't heard from until they "came out" from China which spoke to the primitive nature of China's telecom networks and the paucity of its trade links. Foreign trade and investment were in their infancy, extremely limited in scope and locale, but even so, daringly experimental on the part of Deng who had been purged twice by Mao for not being sufficiently leftist.

---

2 The so-called Gang of Four was organized by Jiang Qing at Mao's command to lead mass campaigns to bring down the detested rivals who had pushed him to the "second rank" after Mao's prior mass movement, the Great Leap Forward (1958-1961), resulted in the death through starvation of tens of millions of Chinese. The Gang of Four spearheaded the worst depredations of Mao's final and most extreme leftist movement, the Cultural Revolution.

3 During the Great Leap Forward, the Chinese economy and society were reorganized along radical, collectivist lines. The purpose was to rapidly increase the production of both food and steel. Villages or parts of a village were given the red and leftist designation "production teams." "Production brigades" consisted of a number of production teams, and production brigades in turn were grouped into "communes." The result was a catastrophic collapse of agriculture and the production of millions of tons of useless iron and steel in backyard furnaces.

China as it is in 2015 or even as it was in 2000 was far from inevitable in 1980, not to say unlikely in the extreme. There were 5,000 automobiles in Beijing and a few times that many telephones, all reserved for official-dom. Electricity was in such short supply that the small dwellings and stores on the two-lane road from Beijing airport to the city had at most one light bulb each. Food was still scarce although the regime supplied the cities with most of whatever was available. In winter, the street corners in Beijing were piled high with mountains of cabbage which seemed bountiful until you realized that was the only supply of the only vegetable that the masses would get to eat until Spring. Private property was barely recognized, and in most cases anyway, the most one could aspire to were the "three treasures": an electric fan, a watch, and a bicycle. People worked six and one-half days per week and wore one of three colors: blue for workers and peasants, green for soldiers, gray for bureaucrats, like an impoverished Land of Oz, it seemed.

Radical revolution saturated the senses. Slogans and songs blared from loudspeakers in public places, 24 hours a day on trains. Everywhere, posters of revolutionary heroes, banners and signs proclaiming Mao's infallibility, the greatness of the proletarian dictatorship, the "Four (or six or three or five) 'Yes"s and 'No's'" of the day, the ultimate victory of Maoist Thought, China's unshakeable unity, "like lips and teeth", with North Korea, China's ally in what we call the Korean War and what they call the War to Assist Korea and Resist American Aggression. Every part of society was militarized, from grade school on.

Starting in 1979, Chinese were taught to treat as *shangdi* [gods] those *laowai* [foreigners] they encountered. This was an extraordinary departure from the immediate past when we were depicted as blood-sucking, imperialist demons and vipers, stepped on or beheaded by heroic Chinese. The effectiveness of the regime's abrupt reversal can only be understood if one realizes that we were a complete abstraction to virtually all Chinese. Very few Westerners went to China for any reason, and those who did were carefully walled off from the masses. Perceptions thus were quite malleable; overnight, demons and vipers metamorphosed into gods, *yanguizi* [foreign devils] became *waibin* [foreign guests]. Then again, the depth of this change in image was shallow. The masses still were fed plenty of anti-Western propaganda that taught suspicion, humiliation, revenge.

Strict distance from foreigners was the norm. Few Chinese were not familiar with the ultimate Maoist insult and crime: "running dog of the imperialists." If Chinese wanted to approach you on the street, they did so furtively, walking along with you to appear as though they were an officially assigned guide, never even agreeing to stop for tea, or to sit down anywhere other than in a park for a few minutes. All they wanted to do was to practice their English and satisfy their curiosity, but they knew that they could be severely punished if they were found out. They felt watched and constrained, and they were.

Even Chinese assigned to your project were not permitted to visit you in your hotel room, and the stern, eagle-eyed floor wardens stationed on every floor ensured strict adherence to this rule. Virtually all contact with Chinese counterparts was limited to group banquets, group tours of possible business locations, group excursions, group meetings. But for all the limitations, good will often shone through the stilted circumstances. In my very first formal meeting in Beijing, at a ministry, I found myself holding hands with my host, a high-ranking official whom I had met in the US, the two of us sitting side by side in a reception room at the head of a large array of people, everyone seated in thickly upholstered armchairs with antimacassars on the arms and backs. That was the way things were then, ritualized, polite, simple, but elegantly genteel, and in a way, genuinely warm.

There was not much Chinese law to learn in 1980. The Cultural Revolution had obliterated the post-1949 Soviet-style legal system, and waves of confiscations of private property and businesses and then collectivization made commercial and property law irrelevant. In 1979, China began an extremely slow process of building a legal framework in order to accommodate foreign investment, starting with a five-page law and a few pages of tax and labor circulars on Chinese-foreign equity joint ventures, the sole permitted vehicle for foreign investment.

At first, this minimal legal set-up contrasted rather pleasantly with the massive amount of law and legal commentary in the US, in corporate and securities practice alone, millions of pages of statutes, regulations, rules, administrative and judicial opinions, law journal articles, and treatises. But with only the brand new fragments of Chinese law, most legal aspects of the joint venture had no clear legal foundation. They would have to be governed by contracts that were carved out of thin air, the only precedent being the one Chinese-foreign joint venture that had been formed at that point.

Added to the legal uncertainties were the endless practical problems that had to be addressed in doing business in China. China's economy not only was centrally planned, it had not emerged from the destitution and near autarchy into which Mao had driven it. Transport, raw materials, skilled labor, office space, everything was in short supply, domestic markets so heavily restricted and export quotas and hard currency so strictly rationed that it was impossible for many businesses to operate, and many gave up before or not long after starting out. The foreign business community that began to enter existed tenuously and only on the margins, a hotel room or two often serving as the China headquarters of large multinationals unless the business was in a highly favored category, and even then there were many limitations on their presence and operations.

I was treated like a head of state, if not a god, because of my host's standing, and because the Chinese government ardently sought my company's investment. In Beijing, I stayed in the Summer Palace, the *Yiheyuan* [the Garden of Nurturing Harmony], in a compound near the foot of *Wanshou Shan* [Longevity Hill]. The only other guests were a few North Koreans who kept to themselves and never ventured forth except for meals when they didn't speak even to each other.

I could scarcely believe it. My Senior Year honors thesis was on the Revolution of 1911 that overthrew the Qing Dynasty and established the Republic. Here I was, staying in the palace the building of which helped to spur that very revolution. I had put aside all my other course work for that thesis, even the winter glee club tour, because I intended it as a tribute to Mary Wright, a sign that even though I was not following the path she wanted for me I was completely serious about Chinese history. Jonathan Spence graded it a 95, and it also won a prize, so I always hoped that the thesis convinced her. But I knew that it did not console her. The last time I met with her, when I was in law school and told her that I had begun to study Chinese language, which she had been urging me to do for years, she responded, with resignation in her voice and in the way she looked out the window and flicked her cigarette: "Maybe you will have a use for it some day." Now that I finally had a use for "it", Chinese language, and all of my China studies, I prayed that she and Mr. Wright were looking down upon me with satisfaction that in the end they had influenced my life in a profoundly positive way.

The *Yiheyuan* is beautiful and poignant. The last gasp of Chinese imperial splendor, its historical resonances extend to China's bitterest experiences in the nineteenth century, the profoundly humiliating military defeats by foreign powers and the "unequal treaties" pursuant to which China was forced to make vast territorial, commercial, and governmental concessions. The infamous Empress Dowager Ci Xi built the *Yiheyuan* to replace the once-exquisite, eighteenth-century *Yuanmingyuan* [Garden of Perfect Brightness] which lies in ruins nearby, ravaged and ransacked to the last tea cup by the British and French Armies during the Second Opium War (1856-1860). The approach of the British and French sent the ruling Xianfeng Emperor and his court into ignominious flight to Jehol, the Summer Capital. There, the emperor died. Ci Xi, the mother of the new emperor, a minor, ended the war on disadvantageous terms, but she returned to Beijing undisputed ruler of the realm.

To build the *Yiheyuan*, Ci Xi diverted funds that had been earmarked to build a desperately needed modern navy. Instead, Ci Xi gave herself this palace, and to top it off, a large marble pavilion in the shape of a pleasure boat that was "moored" on Kunming Lake within the palace grounds. A few years after the *Yiheyuan* was finished, China suffered its most galling defeat of all, in the Sino-Japanese War of 1894-1895, its inadequate fleet sent to the bottom, huge new territories and concessions gouged out, this time, not by Western powers, but by the Japanese, other Asians, whom the Chinese had regarded with contempt. It is no surprise that the *Yiheyuan* became a symbol of Qing decadence and Ci Xi's cynicism, or that it helped make Ci Xi the second most hated woman in Chinese history.

When I wandered about the *Yiheyuan* during visiting hours, throngs of Chinese tourists gaped at me, the occasional brave soul coming up for a few minutes' close contact, even a photograph. Before 9am and after 5pm, the huge complex was mine alone, and the early dawns and late sunsets of North China in midsummer afforded plenty of time to explore. I walked the gorgeous *Chang Lang* [Long Corridor] that runs for nearly one-half mile along Kunming Lake, strolled around to the Opera House and the Marble Boat and across the elegant bridges over the lake and the canals that lead to it, gazed at the famed Western Hills in the distance, and hiked up Longevity Hill to Cloud-Dispelling Hall, Temple of Buddhist Virtue, Sea of Wisdom Temple.

Even with the dearth of autos, I had at my disposal a car and a driver. The car was a baby blue "Shanghai" sedan, nearly identical to the Dodge that my father bought in 1952, and one of a handful among the few cars there were that were not black. The Summer Palace was located in what then was a suburb, and the ride to meetings in Beijing took me through pastoral scenes, boys and men herding huge ducks and fishing in the endless maze of canals. Peter had told me, "Spend some extra time and practice your Mandarin." I took him at his word and wandered all over Beijing and toured the lovely environs, Fragrant Mountain, the Ming Tombs, Taoist and Buddhist temples, and sections of the Great Wall.

Suburban no longer, for many years now the *Yiheyuan* has been conjoined with Beijing, residential and commercial development creeping right up to the outer side of Longevity Hill.

chapter four

One night in early May 2008, over dinner in a nondescript restaurant in Shanghai, I found myself the audience of a blurt-out. "Q.", a Chinese paralegal at a Western law firm, abruptly announced that he had played a key role in arranging a $3 million bribe to gain official approval of a transaction by an iconic American company.

I had known "Q." since 2006 when I asked him to moonlight for me. Capable and diligent, he spoke fluent and idiomatic English and was excellent at translating lengthy, complex documents, a crucial skill. "Q." also had a finely tuned sense of humor which made working with him fun. Fredric met him several times during his trips to China and was very impressed. It thus came as a great shock that "Q." would bring me face to face with a China that I had known was all around but that I had never encountered directly.

In his delight over his transaction, "Q." apparently had not anticipated my reaction: "How dare you do such a thing? You are supposed to know better. *Taoyan* [Disgusting]. I used to think much better of you."

Feigning to check out the waitress, "Q." looked in her direction, then into his plate, anywhere but at me. After an awkward silence, "Q." took a different tack: "We kept telling the client not to do it. We wrote memos warning them. They wouldn't listen. Anyway, the $3 million doesn't go to the officials themselves, just the shell company."

As "Q." spoke, his face had never looked more sly or more fox-like. I didn't ask who the "we" were, but I responded, in a much louder voice than before: "You can't really think that there is any difference. You just said that the officials are the sole shareholders. Your memos mean nothing. You must resign from this assignment, not facilitate this type of thing."

At that, "Q." dropped all resistance to my scolding, but his wincing and squirming only made him more repulsive, so I tried to lighten the mood with a few remarks about the upcoming Beijing Summer Olympics and 2010 Shanghai Expo. "Q."'s end of the conversation now was limited to grunts and gestures signifying "yes" and "no" or nothing at all. When the dinner came to an end, "Q.", no longer the braggart, slouched out of the restaurant ahead of me and off into the dark. I called after him, with some tinge of remorse for hurting his feelings: "See you after the Olympics." "Q." did not reply. Surely, he was telling himself: "Stupid *laowai*; what does he know?"

The Shanghai air seemed particularly vile that night. Not as bad as in Beijing, not as choking or opaque or filled with sand and yellow soil from the Gobi Desert and the loess plateau of Northwest China, but the garlicky flavors from dinner quickly were overlaid with a coating of hydrocarbons. I paced slowly back and forth, in deep thought.

The Chinese Communists had long since departed from the revolutionary path of *Wei renmin fuwu* [To serve the people], one of Mao's great slogans. Even in the 1980s, wags had added a tag to that one: *ye yao qian* [and payment is required], as the policy of *kaifa kaifang* led to corruption severe enough for it to be one of the main factors behind the 1989 Tiananmen Square protest movement.

Some corruption was inevitable once foreign investment and trade proceeds began pouring into China, with its bureaucracy notable for legions of grossly underpaid officials, with its past decades of the most desperate poverty, with its political and social culture stripped of moral boundaries by the Communists' endless, savage political campaigns and movements that killed tens of millions of people, and with foreigners hungry for deals and every bit as tempted to offer a bribe as Chinese officials may have been to ask for one.

China's accession in 2001 to the World Trade Organization (WTO) gave corruption a big boost because of the vastly increased flow of money into China. It also was an historic mistake from the standpoint of the interests of the US. As much as I wanted to see improved and increased US-China relationships of all kinds, it was clear, once the terms and timing of accession became known after the fact, that this structure was being built on sand and that China would be the big winner and the Western countries the big losers.

At the heart of the deal was China's promise to implement Rule of Law, the foundation of WTO, and therein lay the most basic flaw, the inherent contradiction between Rule of Law and Chinese Communism. Even with the change from Mao's egalitarianism and communalism to Deng's "socialist market economy," and his seemingly capitalistic slogan, *Zhi fu guangrong* [To get rich is glorious], no one was even talking about putting the two real power centers behind the government, the Communist Party and the People's Liberation Army, under any laws at all. And no provision was made to remove Chinese courts from the control of the Party's political and legal committees or to institute an independent judiciary. The argument of the proponents of accession that WTO membership by itself would "force" China to become "like the West" was irresponsible and foolish. Only stringent requirements and enforceable penalties for noncompliance, not the proponents' imagined triumph of free-market capitalism, could have made China begin to approach a Rule of Law system, but the terms of China's WTO accession effectively gave the regime carte blanche.

China did make an apparent assault on corruption that convinced some even if the methodology, especially the executions, left others aghast. And compared with 1980, when there literally were no laws or lawyers or courts at all, by 2001 and much more so by 2008, China seemed to have come some distance in creating a legal system. New laws and regulations and rules poured out at every level of government, and an extensive and rapidly growing Chinese bar had formed with legal professionals as skilled and sophisticated as any in the West, many of them trained in the West. *Neibu* [secret, internally published regulations] still operated in the background, more so in transactions in sensitive, restricted sectors, less so in more open parts of the economy, some of which good connections would allow you to see, some of which perhaps you never got to see, or even know about. But overall, deals could be negotiated with increased clarity.

For all the rumors and official reports about corruption, it did not yet seem ubiquitous or inevitable. I had done many deals in the provinces, and the local authorities were so anxious for foreign investment that absolutely no bribe seemed necessary to get those done. My recent work was focused on certain key sectors in which the state- and Party-owned entities seemed inherently immune to corruption. Ensconced in their colossal bastions guarded by soldiers with stern expressions and fixed bayonets stationed every few paces even inside these compounds, these entities were subject to a high level of scrutiny. The clients were leading

US companies known for their ethical standards, the deals were solid, and the economic interests on each side clear and valid.

The fall of Chen Liangyu, the Shanghai party chief, in 2006 was a clue that corruption was getting extreme, but on the other hand, it was not uncommon for political foes to be eliminated on trumped up charges. In the past few years, I had spent much more time in the US than previously, so perhaps I was not as current on such things as I otherwise might have been, and maybe that is why I was so shocked by what "Q." had just told me. Until that dinner with "Q.", I had never heard or seen anything that caused me to have anything other than respect for my Chinese colleagues and the governmental officials with whom I dealt. I socialized with them, went on family outings. I felt that I knew many of them well. But now, with "Q."'s bragging about his bribe, the charmed circle in which I had thought I lived was breached. To hear directly about a bribe by a US company was bad enough, but to have a Western-trained Chinese paralegal, someone with whom I had worked closely, tell me that he was facilitating a bribe was deeply unsettling, and from the standpoint of one who had always wished China well, a betrayal of the best aspects, the best hopes of China, the future of China itself.

I asked myself whether my own clients had been giving bribes all along. I had advised several on complicated legal issues stemming from absconding or corrupt local managers and sales personnel, but these matters did not involve senior management and were dealt with properly. At the level of transactions that I had helped to negotiate, no, how could that be! They all worked far too hard. Why would anyone spend endless hours in marathon negotiating sessions over piles of documents, sometimes for years, if the whole thing could be done with a bribe? And many deals that came along were not feasible for some reason and simply cratered; others could not get official approval because they were not in permitted sectors or of a type that could be approved in a particular sector. I had recently had two media licensing deals just about to close, only to have the Chinese licensees suddenly decide that they really did not want licenses, rather joint ventures with the foreign content owners which was strictly prohibited by Chinese law. "Maybe they couldn't agree on the bribe," I suddenly thought.

In hindsight, "Q."'s revelation was indicative of the situation then and predictive of the future. In 2008, far from receding, corruption was gathering much greater force than ever. But few people then could have imagined the extent to which corruption was taking hold at the pinnacle of the Party, government, and military, that China was becoming, perhaps had become, a Red Kleptocracy.

China's response to the global financial crisis that exploded in September 2008 would remove any doubt about China's direction in this regard. As China's financial markets crashed, the bloated economy threatened to come to a screeching halt. The Chinese government stemmed the panic with an immense financial stimulus, Chinese markets bottomed in November, and fairly quickly the economy resumed its vertiginous growth rate, though at ever greater cost. Opportunists waxed stronger than ever, corruption went parabolic.

The Ministry of Railways was merely one of many epicenters of corruption. Officials from the minister to local bureau chiefs stole incredible amounts from the limitless sums that the government threw at constructing China's high-speed rail network. As early as 2006, the railway minister's own brother (who had worked in a provincial railway bureau) received a suspended death sentence for graft, but that did nothing to slow down the free-for-all or even damage the minister's position until several catastrophic train crashes in 2011-2012 led to exposés about his billions and harem of mistresses.

It also was in 2012 that *The New York Times* and *Bloomberg* published extensive reports on the fortunes amassed by the families of top leaders, "Grandpa" Wen Jiabao (the mild-mannered "reformist" premier whose wife became known as the Diamond Queen of China) and Xi Jinping (the presumptive next president and general secretary of the Party), ultimately in the USD billions and hundreds of millions, respectively.

These reports were immediately squelched in China and the offending publications cowed into not releasing more stories said to have been ready to go.

In May 2008, these reports and the Neil Heywood murder were more than three years in the future. As I gazed at the lights of the Shanghai skyline, it did not occur to me that I could be in danger because of what "Q." had just told me. Instead, I thought about how much things had changed since 1980 when there were only grass fields and farms across the Huangpu River, when the Peace Hotel and the art deco buildings on the Bund cast the only, much more minimal glow on the waterfront, when hotel employees would race after you to the airport if you left a pencil behind.

Now, the stinking air showed the physical price that China was paying for its latest great leap forward. Having caught pneumonia twice when I lived in Beijing, I shuddered at inhaling any more of the only slightly less toxic Shanghai brew. I caught a cab and returned to my apartment and a few days later flew back to San Francisco as planned, to avoid the hordes of tourists about to descend on Shanghai on their way to or from the Beijing Olympics.

chapter five

In 1992, three years after his bloody Tiananmen Square crackdown, which resulted in economic stagnation and a freeze of Western investment,

Deng Xiaoping made his famous "Southern Patrol" to Shenzhen and Shanghai, where he announced a revitalization of economic reforms and development plans. China immediately roared back into action, and the world piled back in. I read the signals, too. I mostly had been performing opera since the mid-1980s, but now I made another sharp turn in direction. I worked intensively on my Chinese and studied the considerable amount of Chinese law that had been enacted. Soon, I began to consult and do strategic planning for technology multinationals that were setting up in China, or considering it, and that led me to spend more and more of each year traveling the length and breadth of China. Like everyone else, I hoped that China's new direction also would mean an improvement in human rights, and, in fact, after some time it did, for a brief time.

China in 1992 was not a great deal more developed than in 1980, and the opportunities were even greater because now there was more structure legally, many more areas of the economy and the country, though by no means all, were open to foreign investment, and China had begun to put in necessary infrastructure. The gross domestic product soared, although from a very low base; even by the end of the decade, China was still quite poor. The distance it still had to go, the primitiveness of so much of the country even in 1999 were epitomized for me by a tool manufacturer in Yangjiang in southern Guangdong Province from which I was sourcing items for a major US retail chain. It took most of a day to get there from Hong Kong, a ferry that departed infrequently across the Pearl River Delta to Jiangmen, then a very long taxi ride on narrow roads. The manufacturer had a fax machine, which was progress to be sure, but they ran it off a generator that was powered by bicycle. Every time I wanted to send to them, I had to call and then wait for them to crank up the electricity.

With the new millennium and the prospect of China's accession to WTO, international law firms geared up for an onslaught of new China business. Suddenly, job offers abounded. I accepted one with a New York firm in their Beijing office. Fredric was in favor of the move. I would have to go to San Francisco on business, and he planned to come to China often. In June 2000, twenty years after my first trip to China, nearly to the day, I settled down to the life of an expat.

Vast parts of China still were undeveloped or underdeveloped, but by now Beijing had many of the trappings of a modern global capital. The office was in the elegant China World Trade Center, so I rented a flat in one of the residential towers in that complex, with a panoramic view of Beijing, three minutes' walk to work through an upscale shopping center. The China World Apartments was one of the most desirable addresses in Beijing, but the proximity to the office was the biggest draw for me. Traffic was a horrible nightmare even in 2000, fifteen years and 5,000,000 cars ago; a short distance could take hours. The mere thought of Beijing brought with it memories of being stuck for endless, indefinite periods of time without the slightest idea of when I might arrive at my appointments, agonizing over keeping people waiting for me or having them leave before I even arrived. And the traffic jams were only part of the commuting misery. Getting a taxi in rush hour required heroic gestures, and they were called for by the smog and the gruesome climate which made walking to mass transit, waiting outside, and cycling extremely unappealing, what with brutal winters, mud storms and sand storms in Spring, and Summer temperatures much higher than the 39 degrees Celsius routinely reported (because if the reading exceeded 40, factory workers had to be sent home.)

For all its disadvantages, I really loved Beijing. I had already spent a great deal of time there and knew it quite well. On weekends and holidays, I enjoyed the many wonderful things to do. In fine weather and decent air (and there was some of both in Spring and Fall), there were magnificent parks, with their exquisite, fragrant cherry trees and lilacs; the colorful *hutongs* [alleys] in the remaining fragments of Old Beijing; the leafy embassy districts. In all kinds of weather, there were endless teashops, flea markets, and museums. It was great to be part of the vibrant expat community and an active Yale alumni crowd, to enjoy the regular company of Chinese friends made over the years, to make many new ones, of many nationalities, through business and socially, the way contacts beget contacts. Some of my friends also loved opera and classical music, and we spent rainy weekend hours listening to CDs and watching DVDs. I gave a few performances of my own, concerts at embassies and clubs through the excellent accompanist I had found.

Like most foreigners in China who could afford it, I hired a housekeeper, or *ayi*. A good *ayi* is a factotum par excellence, the steward of all domestic matters, from house cleaning to paying bills to running errands to buying food to cooking to doing the laundry. Her paramount function is to superintend the food supply and ward off everything from rampant adulteration to outright poisoning. Next in importance, in 2000, was paying bills because they had to be paid in cash in person at specific hours on specific days of the month, at addresses all over town--the electricity company, the gas company, the telephone company, the mobile phone company, the bottled water company. No one accepted personal checks, accounts were not online. In fact, few Chinese owned computers, and China had only just begun to develop an Internet.

Beijing Ayi came recommended by a colleague for whom she also worked. She was in her early-mid 60s, short and dark, with very pleasant features and the gruff humor and manner of a native Beijinger. She spoke the earthy Beijing dialect, laced with growls and burrs, and magnificent Standard Mandarin, her tones crystal clear, never mincing, never piercing. After a year or more she told me that she was a Manchu on both sides, not a Han Chinese. I was fascinated and wondered which "banner"[4] she belonged to, but I never asked because she told me that she was registered as a Han. She at least valued Han status over the special favors given to Manchus as one of the 55 officially recognized minority peoples.[5]

She had retired from her human resources position at a state-owned knitting factory and had acquired property, her own two-bedroom, two-bath apartment in a pleasant district not far from the center of Beijing. She lived there with the *Lao Tongzhi* [Old Comrade] as she referred to her husband. She invested in the nascent Chinese stock market, apparently successfully. *Women hen gaoxing* [We're very happy]! she told me early on about that.

---

4 Under the Qing (or Manchu) Dynasty, the Manchu population was organized into the Eight Banners which were social-military formations.
5 Such favors included exemption from the hated one-child policy that Deng Xiaoping implemented to control the explosive birth rate that Mao had expressly encouraged.

Beijing *Ayi* was a fine and forthright person, generous, intelligent, fiercely loyal, and marvelous company. To Chinese, calligraphy is the hallmark of learning and cultivation, and her calligraphy was exemplary. She was a proud Communist Party member. The Party had meant everything to her, education, job, improved living standards. I often thought that she was an example of the best that the Party produced, and knowing her, and many fine people in the Chinese government and professions, was enough to make me waver slightly in my distaste for and distrust of the regime. She had a fine singing voice and loved music. When I practiced for recitals, I was very glad to have her critical ear. She was a masterful chef and worked up elegant dinners that gave me plenty of *mianzi* [face] with my Chinese and Western guests.

Beijing *Ayi* actually repeated the Party line, ["foreigners are gods"], and decided to dress me and Fredric as Chinese princes. An excellent seamstress, she made for each of us several sets of robes of an extraordinarily beautiful, sapphire-colored silk with embroidered gold medallions. When the summit of the Asia-Pacific Economic Cooperation forum (APEC) was held in Shanghai in 2001, she summoned Tailor Wu to create an exact replica of the *zongtongfu* [presidential garment], a lined silk Mandarin jacket that China's leader, Jiang Zemin, gave to the assembled heads of state. Among the official colors, I chose the emerald-green. Once I wore the *zongtongfu* to a party in New York City and showed it to my mother; she was so thrilled with it that I asked Tailor Wu to make the same jacket for her.

Beijing *Ayi* introduced me to her stepson and her older sister and brother-in-law, lovely people, especially the sister. The sister had many serious ailments, so many that it was amazing that she could keep going, but she had one of the kindest faces I have ever seen. We visited them at their apartment in Asian Games Village in the North of Beijing. In 1993, it was an expanse of raw, concrete high rises, but now it was filled with mature landscaping and locust trees that gave the place an entirely different and very pleasant aspect.

I came to love Beijing *Ayi* deeply, in a Platonic way, and I made sure to repay her generosity. The only moment of discord came during the Hainan plane incident in 2001 when a Chinese pilot died in a collision of his fighter jet with a US spy plane. Fresh from a Party meeting, Beijing *Ayi* marched into my apartment waving her finger at me, intoning:

Meiguo buhao. Meiguo hen huai [America is not good. America is very bad]!

I calmed her down: *Buliaoliaozhi* [Not talk-talk it, i.e., let's not discuss it].

We never did speak about it again even though the diplomatic crisis dragged on for weeks, at the top of the news broadcast every night, as the Chinese took their good time dismantling the plane and making the US sweat over the return of our plane crew.

Originally, Beijing *Ayi* worked for me three half-days per week which was more than I needed. After a few months, entirely at her initiative, she was at my apartment three whole days, and then almost every day once she left the employ of the colleague who had recommended her. The colleague had adopted a baby and needed full-time help and offered the job to Beijing *Ayi*. I told her that she should take it, but she announced:

Wo pianxiang ni [I lean toward you].

So, I raised her salary to compensate. But the money wasn't the issue. I had been becoming nervous at the tone of things, and became much more so when she began hinting, and then stated outright, that she wanted to marry me once the Old Comrade passed away. He was very ill and much older than she, and the way she described it, he had one foot in the grave and the other on a banana peel. *Yihou* [afterward], she would say when she wanted to be more subtle.

At first, I tried to take it as a joke, and also counted on the durability of the Old Comrade, but one day she told me:

Wo jie tongyi [my older sister agrees]!

Thereupon she threw me on the couch, jumped on me, and tickled me. I knew then that I had to limit the time that I spent with her and her family because I was terrified of misleading her and hurting her feelings.

When I first met her, I never imagined that Beijing *Ayi* would form a romantic attachment, but since Chinese society is notably homophobic, people such inveterate gossips and snitches, right at the outset I told her that my "cousin" would be visiting Beijing often on his own business and that he would be staying with me. Since Fredric and I don't share the same last name or look remotely similar, I was careful to tell her that he was my *biaodi* [maternal cousin], that he resembled his father as I did mine, and that we were very close because we had grown up together.

I never did find out for sure what she thought my relationship with Fredric was, but the story seems to have convinced her, because she never so much as batted an eyelash whenever the subject of *Didi* [younger brother or younger cousin] came up. In fact, she liked *Didi* a lot and always brightened at the news of a visit by him. Whereupon, she would go into overdrive with special preparations, making sure to prepare the dishes that he liked, knitting an extra sweater, sprucing up the apartment with flowers.

Whatever she thought, whatever she hoped, she never flagged in her devotion to my interests or showed an iota less friendship. In 2002, I developed a nearly crippling back problem. Beijing *Ayi* was terribly concerned and inquired everywhere for a good acupuncturist. We went to five or six, all over Beijing, including one in Asian Games Village who had helped her sister, but none of them seemed to be able to help me.

Dr. Wang treated me in my apartment. He used huge needles that looked as though they came from Beijing *Ayi*'s knitting basket. These he would plunge into my neck and back. I endured four visits of the prescribed course of ten until, before the fifth, I telephoned Beijing *Ayi* from my office to tell her to pay Dr. Wang, that I couldn't face another session with him. It was a sign of my great respect for her, and of my desperation, that I got through more than the first minute with him, as he asked:

Baifen zhi duoshao shi teng; baifeng zhi duoshao shi ma [What percentage pain; what percentage numb]?

I, barely able to emit a sound, the tiniest movement in my neck sheer agony:

Baifen zhi bai shi teng; baifen zhi ling shi ma. [100% pain; 0% numb].

After ten minutes of awful pain, numbness did indeed set in, but without noticeable benefit.

On visits to my Western-trained doctor in the Kerry Center, across Guanghua Road from the China World, I needed more than the split second that the pedestrian-unfriendly traffic lights allowed. So, as soon as the light turned, Beijing *Ayi* would stride out into the middle of the four lane, two-way traffic, plant herself in the cross walk, extend her arms out fully to each side, palms up, and in a commanding voice announce:

Nimen zhuyi: Waibin laile [All of you, pay attention: a foreign guest has arrived]!

The traffic would come to a halt for as long as it took me to hobble across the street.

So much negative information has come out about China in recent years that now I sometimes wonder whether Beijing *Ayi* was the pure friend she certainly seemed to be, or whether, like so many Chinese, she was obligated by the Party to inform regularly on any foreigner for whom she worked, including me. Unless she was taught to plant malware on my computer in order to extract client information, it would not have mattered. There never was anything to inform about. Something deep inside me still wants to believe that she was too principled to spy on someone she knew trusted her and that she still would be. But whatever the situation then, with the overall relationship between the US and China now more tense than at any time since the Korean War, for sure she would be more suspicious of me and I of her if we were getting to know each other now.

From the standpoint of a more open society, the late 1990s and early 2000s were the most hopeful time in China since Liberation, as the Communists refer to their victory over the Nationalists in 1949. It was exhilarating to be immersed in this vast, still-exotic country that was bursting with energy, both individual and societal. People expressed their views much more openly, you could visit with them in their homes, you could befriend officials purely for friendship, you could travel freely almost everywhere, all of which were unthinkable when I started to go to China. Telephones and even cell phones had become commonplace. The Internet was beginning to give people access to information and a voice that they had never had. The all-intrusive Great Firewall that censors the Chinese Internet so drastically now was planned from the inception, but in the early years it was imperfect and relatively lightly used. The Beijing Olympics win in 2001 offered a promise, though vague, that the regime would respect human rights. Jiang Zemin was advancing his Three Represents theory which, as a matter of Chinese Communist doctrine, opened membership in the Party to business people who would have been anathematized and imprisoned or executed as bourgeois opportunists and class enemies in the not-very-distant past.

But for the same reason that WTO would not lead to a Chinese economy based on Rule of Law, all these glimmerings of personal freedoms would turn out to be a mirage, no more real than the bushes at the China World and other key spots in Beijing that were spray painted green in the middle of December to create a verdant appearance for the final Olympic Committee inspection tour. The Communist Party can not tolerate any limitation on its absolute dominance of the individual and of social and political life any more than it can tolerate any limitation on its control of the economy or legal system. It was a grievous error, one in which I shared to some extent, to imagine that anything approximating an open society could develop more than superficially in a system where something as bloody and traumatic as the nationwide Tiananmen atrocities remained unacknowledged, unaccounted for, and un-redressed, where the merest mention of them brought down the most extreme wrath of the Party, where people routinely were thrown into jails and labor camps and mental hospitals for speaking out publicly, for petitioning for compensation for illegally appropriated land, for practicing a peaceful religion, for saying anything remotely favorable about democracy, for advocating for human rights or even for Rule of Law itself.

chapter six

W hile still residing in Beijing, for most of six months in 2002 I worked in Shanghai on a multi-billion dollar infrastructure project. It was extremely complex with many parties and required an inordinate number of governmental approvals, even for China. There were endless committees, sub-committees, and sub-sub-committees on every aspect. The most minor detail or question from government officials would bring everything to a halt as reports were prepared and meetings held to feed or prod the snail-like review process of layer after layer of bureaucracy, up and back down, often late into the night. Sometimes, I imagined that the unseen mandarins worked only after midnight and that was why we sometimes had to work 24 hours per day on the simplest points.

Worse even than the bureaucracy was the veritable Tower of Babel that sprang up at the slightest provocation. I had worked on projects in many places in China where the local dialect was distinct enough from Standard Mandarin that it might as well have been a second language, but everyone always tried to accommodate people not from the locale by speaking Mandarin as best they could in negotiations. Shanghai is different, Shanghainese do not like to speak anything but Shanghainese, and although there are as many theories as theorizers about Chinese languages, Shanghainese, with its toneless-seeming staccato, has always seemed to me a completely distinct language, not a dialect of Mandarin.

In meetings for this deal, there were always simultaneous conversations in different dialects of Mandarin and in Shanghainese, and not necessarily on the same subjects, by anywhere from 10-35 people in the room at any one time. The ground rule was to speak some type of Mandarin, but even in the course of a relatively orderly meeting, after five minutes, the Shanghai contingent instinctively lapsed into some part Mandarin, some part Shanghainese, the longer and the more heated the discussion, the greater their resort to Shanghainese. It literally *shangle wode naojin* [strained my brain tendons] to keep track of everything that was going on.

It was not a plus that the meetings took place in Pudong New District, where I also stayed to avoid commuting to the meetings. Brand new, bleak, and growing like Topsy, an endless expanse of ugly new construction across the Huangpu River from Old Shanghai. It was still less a plus that at dinners hosted by them, the Shanghainese ordered meals entirely of raw shellfish - oysters, crabs, shrimps, mussels, periwinkles, sea urchins, sea cucumbers.

I had forced myself out of politeness to swallow some pretty gruesome items in China, the worst being whatever was in the ceremonial bite that I had no choice but to fish out of a hot pot in Chengdu into which numerous items along with dog meat had been thrown, avoiding swallowing until I could spit it out. In Yichang, 1000 miles up the Yangtze River, the big treat was an odoriferous, leathery, but cooked, river turtle shell. There I got away with plucking off a minuscule sliver of the sickeningly white flesh, tossing it down my throat with a particularly raw *baijiu* [white spirits] to kill any microbes, and, as raucous applause awarded my minimal act of daring, passing it under the table to the person to my right who split it with the person to his right, the two of them to gnaw the thing happily down to its struts.

But eating raw shellfish from the massively polluted rivers and coasts of China seemed so recklessly lethal that it was inconceivable for me even to make a show of lifting it to my lips. No amount of hectoring by the others at the table could get me to overcome the gag reflex. When a few cooked but oily, bony, fleshless fish from the same ghastly waters would be served for my benefit, only extreme measures sufficed, such as surreptitiously tossing them under the table or wrapping them in paper napkins and throwing them in the toilet. That was in 2002; the pollution levels then, for example in the Huangpu River, which supplies Shanghai's drinking water, were nothing compared to 2013 when another eleven years of ever increasing discharges of poisonous effluents were crowned by the procession of 30,000 diseased pig carcasses down the Huangpu, right through the center of Shanghai.

In 2005, I was working on my own out of Beijing and San Francisco when a Europe-based law firm offered me a job in Shanghai. At that point, business was slow. My biggest pending assignment, as an arbitrator in a large China-related case in New York City, had barely begun, and the case might have settled at any point. I was not very enthusiastic about living in Shanghai. Basically a creation of nineteenth-century colonialism, it held little historical interest compared to Beijing with its thousands of years of history. Most importantly, most of my friends and contacts in China lived there. But, I thought, why not get to know the commercial heart of China better.

Beijing *Ayi* helped me in every way to prepare for the move, including psychologically, or at least she tried. She told me, with genuine concern in her voice:

Shanghai ren hen hua [Shanghai people are very slippery].

I waved her away with a laugh. I knew Shanghai's reputation for tough and clever business people, but I had been a New Yorker for much of my life, so that didn't scare me. And I said to myself, "Chinese always bad mouth people from other provinces."

The office was in Jing An District, in Old Shanghai which I had always liked. I found an apartment in the former French Concession, on Julu Road which is graced by art deco lane houses, mansions, and extravagantly beautiful plane trees, ten minutes' walk from the office on spiffy Nanjing West Road. Best of all, I could avoid Shanghai's version of commuter hell, for traffic jams there were at least as epic as those in Beijing, especially bad in the long monsoon seasons when you faced eternal waits for taxis and then endless rides, or being baked alive in unbearable humidity on public transit packed impossibly densely with people.

There were two nice walks to work. One went through the arches and gates of the lane houses, past marble placards that announced the names of the many artists and writers who had lived there during the great era of pre-World War II Shanghai. The other took me past the huge former mansion of A.P. Møller, the Danish ship magnate, and the jewel-like Shanghai Exhibition Center, a 1950s gift from the Soviets that is surprisingly different from overbearing Stalinist "wedding cake" architecture.

The landlady on Julu Road recommended one "N." as my *ayi*. "N." was a terrible cook; after two inedible dinners, I put her on the phone with Bejing *Ayi* who explained what to buy and how to cook it. "N."'s cuisine improved instantly, and I never said a critical word to the landlady. But two weeks after "N." started, just as I was becoming accustomed to her, the landlady called to announce that her "church elder" had informed her, *Neige "N." Ayi, you wenti* [There is a problem with that "N." *Ayi*].

Wenti. A problem. A word that appears seemingly in every other sentence in Chinese. In this case, it could have meant that "N." was anything from a slacker to an axe-murderer. During more politically radical periods, it often meant a flaw in class background.

["What's the problem?"] I asked.

The Landlady: ["I can't risk it. "N." must go."]

"*She* can't risk *it*!" I thought. "Risk what? How typical of this country. Denounce this woman with unspecified charges, no evidence, just a *wenti*, give her no chance to defend herself." Then, I wondered: "Is the landlady a member of an 'underground church'"? Are they afraid that "N." is a government spy?"

Despite my resentment at this summary verdict, I bowed to reality. *Mei banfa* [Nothing can be done about it], the refrain of conversations in China. The landlady had introduced "N.", and she would hold me responsible if anything went wrong. *Mei banfa*, for sure this time.

The landlady came downstairs to my apartment to advise "N." of her dismissal and then handed her a 100 *renminbi* banknote (about USD 12.) Disgusted by the landlady's cheapness and arrogance, not concerned that she would think me a fool and take offense at her loss of face, I ran to my bedroom, grabbed some money and gave "N." two months' salary. After "N." left, the landlady did scold me, but she turned right back to business and recommended her own *ayi*. That *ayi* became for me, forever, "the Shanghai *ayi*".

chapter seven

The Shanghai *ayi* was in her early 50s, slender, medium height, pale complexion, perfectly aligned eyes, delicate mouth, an oval face only slightly careworn, lustrous black hair with subtle auburn highlights. Her voice was rich and her laugh melodious and charming. Ten or fifteen years younger, she still would have been a classic *jiangnan meinü* [beauty from South of the Yangtze].

The Shanghai *ayi*'s cooking was much simpler than Beijing *Ayi*'s, but very tasty. She quickly learned my likes and dislikes and the limits of my daring. She would bring back aprons-full of still-warm eggs from her best farm lady, and she loved to describe in detail how she managed to get the freshest vegetables, cuts of pork or beef without a sliver of fat or gristle, the plumpest chicken. She thought to quickly establish her bona fides by keeping the most absurdly detailed accounts of household expenses, down to the last Chinese cent—not that I ever bothered to review her sheaves of receipts and lists written with her ragged, coarse calligraphy.

About three months after the Shanghai *ayi* began to work for me, I came home to find her there, distraught. Her husband, Mr. Z., had been riding in a van that was broadsided where he was sitting, and he was near death. But he survived, and some weeks later, when he was released from the hospital, I insisted on doing the proper thing and visiting Mr. Z.

The Shanghai *ayi* lived with Mr. Z. and their 25-year-old son, "YY", in a rented hovel, about 250 square feet, in part of an attic of a carved up *shikumen* (a style of row house) in Hongkou District, the former Japanese Concession, across Suzhou Creek from the Bund and Old Shanghai, on a narrow street off Sichuan North Road. The hike up the four flights of steep, uneven stairs, so dimly lighted and so cluttered with belongings of every description, and so rickety, that the next step easily could be your last, was a walk through the lives of seven or eight families, 25 or 30 people, crammed into a dwelling originally meant for one moderately well-off family. Baskets, bags, and clothes hung on poles suspended into every available space in the stairwell. Even the landings seemed to harbor entire households.

I was amazed at the way the Shanghai *ayi*'s family used their space. On the right side as you entered was a tiny sink, a counter, and child-sized table and chairs. The bed of Mr. Z. and the Shanghai *ayi*, was on the left side, a raised wooden pallet with a thin mattress. At the foot of the bed was a jerry-built structure, shaped like an elongated oven, maybe half as wide as the bed, inside of which "YY" slept. The tiny door to the enclosure didn't seem nearly large enough for someone the size of "YY" to crawl through, and I couldn't imagine how he endured a Shanghai summer sleeping in there, as if the rest of the apartment wouldn't be insufferable enough. At the far end of this space was a door to a shared balcony where there were several small stoves, each belonging to a family, and a communal toilet.

The stricken Mr. Z., who I had never met, lay wrapped up completely immobile, identical in appearance to an Egyptian mummy. Every bone in his body was broken, so the Shanghai *ayi* said, and so it seemed. Mr. Z. could barely speak, and a ceremonial visit was all that he could manage. As I left the awful sight, I pushed the 10,000 *renminbi* (about USD 1,200 then) that I had brought with me into the pocket of the Shanghai *ayi*'s apron. She didn't resist very strongly. Who would in such a circumstance? She thanked me profusely. *Nali, nali. Shi wo yinggai zuode. Ni xian zhaogu nide jiangfu ba* [It's nothing, nothing. It's what I ought to do. Now, go take care of your husband].

A few weeks later, Fredric arrived in Shanghai. *Didi* [younger cousin] had already met the Shanghai *ayi*, and he wanted to pay a visit to Mr. Z. By this time, Mr. Z.'s bruised face was partially visible, and he was able to speak, although he still could not get out of bed. We invited the Shanghai *ayi* and "YY" to go to dinner, Mr. Z. expressing much pleasure at the mention of the leftovers that the Shanghai *ayi* promised to bring back. After saying goodbye to him, we each pressed on the Shanghai *ayi* whatever cash we had on us, several thousand *renminbi* each.

The Shanghai *ayi* proudly brought us, her foreign friends, to her favorite seafood haunt, down the street from her place, a humid and noisy den of fish tanks and shallow pools, tables lined up alongside the swimming fish, a leaky tangle of hoses and pipes ensuring that the muddy water sloshing all over the floor kept well ahead of the sporadic efforts by the staff to contain it. All ocean-caught fish, she assured us. Better than from a river anyway, and a single dose of cooked toxins wasn't likely to kill us.

After a lengthy consultation with the waiter, the Shanghai *ayi* selected what she said was the best specimen in the place. The waiter pulled an enormous fish out of one of the tanks and presented it to us flipping around crazily in a pail. Dinner consisted of courses made from that fish. Handmade fish balls that seemed to have been extruded from a chopping machine, lightly fried fish fillets, slices of fish sautéed with different sauces and vegetables, and soup, all delicious. As the last of the dishes were cleared away, "YY" downed two beers in rapid succession in celebration of a great dinner. Then the Shanghai *ayi* made a great fuss. The remains of the fish, head, tail, skin, bones, organs, had disappeared! Where was it all? The staff jumped to accommodate and produced a vat of seemingly unrecognizable goo. The Shanghai *ayi* was sure that it was from our fish. However, the restaurant did not have a container to take it away in, so while we stood guard over this treasure, she ran home and up and down those perilous stairs, re-appearing shortly carrying a huge pot. The waiter loaded the stuff in, and then we said good night.

Mr. Z'.s accident wasn't the only time that I opened my wallet for the Shanghai *ayi*. A few months later, she arrived at my apartment in tears. She told that she had left an envelope containing 20,000 *renminbi* in a taxi on the way back to the landlady. It was the month's rent from some of the landlady's real estate empire that the Shanghai *ayi* was responsible for collecting. Without a word, I got out 10,000 *renminbi* and put it in the Shanghai *ayi*'s pocket book. She wiped her tears and went upstairs to see the landlady. "I guess that Mrs. W. won't be letting her off for the other half," I thought, not without a momentary, queasy feeling that the always suspicious landlady might be furious with me once again for setting a bad example with an *ayi*, and maybe justifiably a bit more skeptical about the Shanghai *ayi*'s story. Assuming, that is, that the Shanghai *ayi* even told her that story.

Then, the issue of "YY"'s tuition came up. He needed 5,000 *renminbi* for a "remedial course" of some type. "Who gives this course," I asked. "The professor in charge of his part of the department," said the Shanghai *ayi*. The nickel dropped slowly, and too late. It sounded like a bribe to the professor to give "YY" a passing grade. I regretted giving her that money much more than helping her out with the money she claimed to have lost.

When the lease was up on the apartment, the landlady proposed a modest increase in rent which I accepted. A few days later, two minutes before we were to sign a new lease, she called to demand a much larger increase. I lost my temper. Grabbing up two huge, cheap vases that she had given me as reparations for an expensive piece of porcelain of mine that one of her relatives had broken, I took the stairs to her floor. Banging on her door, I shouted: ["Here, take back this worthless crap."] The sight of her, uncoiffed, shocked looking, beet-red angry, was unnerving.

The Shanghai *ayi*, working through the doorman, quickly located another apartment in the same building on a higher floor with an even better view and for less rent. In fact, the view was magnificent, comprising Julu Road and equally verdant adjacent streets, all the way to Xiangyang Park. The many office towers in the distance framed the entire scene, by day with their mostly interesting architecture, by night with fabulous light shows. I was more than impressed with the Shanghai *ayi*'s resourcefulness.

Around that time, the Shanghai *ayi* announced that she couldn't stand working any longer for the landlady. Too exhausting. The *laotaitai* [old lady] was ungrateful and spoke of nothing but her ailments, how much money she had amassed, the palatial homes in Queens, NY that she had bought for her ungrateful daughters, how she fought non-stop with them and their husbands, how they all hated her, and how the ravenous packs of local relatives forever nipped away at her pocketbook.

I urged the Shanghai *ayi* to stay on with the landlady. I was concerned about her welfare, and it also occurred to me that the landlady would blame me for the loss of her employee, but the Shanghai *ayi* was determined to quit. The three half-days days per week that she worked for me were plenty, but those three half-days soon became five or six, so I increased her salary commensurately. As in Beijing, I hadn't asked for or wanted so much attention, but I believed that both *ayis* were motivated by a fundamental insecurity, a mentality of privation and bitter struggle shaped by the tumultuous past of Chinese society that made many Chinese do everything imaginable to make themselves indispensable to their employer and leave no way in for a competitor. I could think of no way to tell the Shanghai *ayi* to limit her presence.

chapter eight

The Shanghai *ayi* described Mr. Z. as a white-collar employee in some state-owned enterprise that had been a government bureau until the late 1980s. His career had not gone very far, given the way he and his family lived. A year or so after I got to know them, it slipped out that he really was a messenger and that he rode a motorcycle around town for his work. But Mr. Z. had a strong intellectual bent, and he shaped his life around studying classical culture, perfecting his calligraphy, and collecting artifacts such as coins and seals. In China, one's occupation often has nothing to do with one's level of learning, indeed, for people in their 60s like Mr. Z., being an intellectual, with or without formal education, was a ticket to the garbage heap or worse during extremist periods such as the Cultural Revolution. I wondered what happened to Mr. Z. then, because one never asked about such things in China, and no one ever brought it up even though the Shanghai *ayi* often spoke of herself during those times.

I shared some of Mr. Z.'s interests and saw a kindred soul in him. He was trying to keep up his set of US quarters that represent the 50 states. As they were issued, I brought him the latest mint ones each time I returned from San Francisco. In a gesture of friendship that left me nearly speechless, Mr. Z. presented me with a jade seal carved by his old master for me, on all four sides with epigrams and poems and my Chinese name, in magnificent calligraphy. This was the second-to-last seal that the old master would ever make, Mr. Z. said, because he had fallen gravely ill. Mr. Z.

showed me the last such seal, made for Mr. Z. only a few months after mine, and the wavering hand was immediately apparent. *Ganxie wujin, Z. xiansheng. Kezhen shi yige baobei* [Thank you without limit, Mr. Z. It truly is a treasure], I said as I shook his hand.

The Shanghai *ayi* and Mr. Z. introduced me to Mr. and Mrs. L., their best friends. Mr. L. ran some business that he owned, the nature of which was never described. Mrs. L. was a nurse at a local hospital. Soon, I was invited to all the banquets of the family circle, holidays, birthdays, always at a restaurant. Usually, Mr. and Mrs. L. were the hosts, but sometimes they allowed the Shanghai *ayi* and Mr. Z. to *qingke* [be the host], and, rarely, I was allowed to do the honors. The attendees were always those four and "YY", often joined by "YY"'s tutor and his wife and baby, and Mr. and Mrs. L.'s daughter and her boyfriend.

Mr. and Mrs. L. clearly were much better off than Mr. Z. and the Shanghai *ayi*, and I was very touched that Mr. and Mrs. L. treated them as equals. Anxious to give the Shanghai *ayi mianzi* [face], I made sure to refer to her not as "*X. Ayi*" which would have denoted, politely, her status as a servant, but with the diminutive form, *Xiao X.* [Little X.], the way one addresses a younger friend, colleague, or member of a family. In fact, I thought of her more as a friend than an employee.

The tutor occupied a very special place in this group. A native of Lianyungang, a grim industrial port in the north of Jiangsu Province, he had somehow managed to obtain a college degree in Shanghai, not an easy thing for a poor student without a Shanghai *hukou* [residence permit]. "YY" had a *hukou* because he was born in Shanghai and his parents were Shanghai residents, so he had automatic access to Shanghai educational institutions, but like many high school students he needed special help to prepare for the fearsome *gaokao* [university admission exam]. So they invited the tutor to live with them in their tiny space by way of compensating him for teaching "YY". For several years, the tutor slept in "YY"'s oven-shaped sleeping pod, and "YY" slept on the floor, until at last "YY" passed his entrance exams and the tutor got married. The level of self-sacrifice by all four was impressive.

Pleasant people, spirited exchanges completely in Chinese. No one at the table really spoke English except me, and everyone other than me and "YY" was limited to one or two words of English at a time: "very good", "delicious", "yes", "no".

Fredric attended one of these banquets and observed that this was an extended family, its fabric woven of threads of interpersonal ties that remained after the terrible famine of the Great Leap Forward, the near destruction of the traditional family structure during the Cultural Revolution, and Deng Xiaoping's one-child policy. All three of the Chinese families at the table were one-child families, at least at the level of "YY"'s generation and the next, and there were few living siblings at the level of the older generation. It seemed as though they had all sought each other out in lieu of the bevy of brothers, sisters, cousins, uncles, and aunts who would have been at such gatherings but for the Communists' massive social engineering and annihilations.

chapter nine

"YY" was a tall, somewhat gawky version of his mother. The faces of the two were nearly identical except that the Shanghai *ayi's* skin was flawless and "YY"'s was marked with severe acne. They had the same smile and air. Totally under his mother's thumb, he jumped at her slightest command. "YY" liked to tag along on outings to buy things like gifts, electronics, or cameras. I offered "YY" advice on his studies, especially on how to improve his English.

One evening, "YY" called up in tears and asked to go out for a walk. He had fallen in love a few months before and wanted to get engaged, but his parents adamantly disapproved of his girlfriend. I knew that his future meant everything to his parents, so I wanted to help as best I could. It did not take long to see that they had reason to be concerned.

"YY" wept copiously as he described how the girl had taken pity on him and liked him despite his pockmarks and boils.

["She even bought me some cream for my face"], he sobbed.

First, I addressed the skin problem:

["I don't know what sort of cream that is, but I have some facial cleanser from Israel, made with Dead Sea mud, full of minerals that definitely will help your skin."]

It didn't take a doctor to see that "YY"'s skin was too severely ravaged for anything other than surgical procedures to make any major difference, but I wanted to cheer him up. As "YY" grew calmer, I took peppered him with questions, her background, how they had met. It turned out that she came from an even poorer family than "YY"'s.

["How do you know that she really loves you? You have only known each other for a few months."]

["She loves me, I know it,"] "YY" said as his voice choked up again.

["How do you know that you love her?"]

["I know it. She took pity on me."] By now, "YY" was blubbering.

["There are so many opportunists in today's society. Does she have a *hukou*?"]

["No, she's from Jiangsu".]

["YY", how do you know that she doesn't want to marry you for your *hukou*? You don't need someone to take pity on you. You will have your degree in another year, and there will be dozens of girls who will want to marry you."]

["Really?"]

["Really. At least you should wait until you graduate to see how you feel about each other."

["Really?"]

["Yes."]

Then, I drew out what I thought was my trump card, filial piety:

["Your parents have sacrificed so much to give you an education. In the end, you must obey them. You must wait."]

Such advice given by a Chinese during the Cultural Revolution could have been lethal. Confucian thinking and speech were outlawed and children were encouraged, even compelled, to inform against their parents, or, worse, to beat them to death in public if, like Mr. Z., they followed forbidden intellectual pursuits. But times had changed, and Confucius had come back into vogue, superficially anyway.

However, it wasn't Confucius or filial piety that prevailed that night. "YY", it turned out, was not so attached to the girl, and he really wanted to placate his mother and get out of his overly hasty commitment. What better way than to tell the girlfriend that a *laowai* lawyer had told him that it was best to wait to get married? "YY" was off the hook, broad smiles replaced tears, he fairly skipped home. That was the last that I heard about that girlfriend. "YY" for the first time had "rented a *laowai*".

chapter ten

In late 2006, the New York arbitration in which I had been serving for two years went to a final award, a three to zero vote for the parties that had appointed me, a highly unusual result, I later found out. I enjoyed that case tremendously, especially the collegiality of counsel and my fellow arbitrators. So I decided to develop an arbitration practice focused on China.

But there are challenging issues in developing such a practice at a law firm. Legal ethics principles restrict lawyers and law firms from representing a party with interests adverse to those of an existing client. Thus, all potential new business is subject to internal conflicts checks concerning all legal matters handled by all lawyers in all offices at the firm. The larger and more global the law firm, and the larger and more global the clients, the more complex and more numerous the inquiries, and the greater the possibility of there being a potential conflict with a party to an arbitration. If a new matter poses a potential conflict as to any party, further time-consuming procedures must be followed to notify the parties and to obtain their objections to or waivers of the potential conflict. If a party objects, the firm may not accept the new business.

In my arbitration, the parties that appointed me were two huge insurance companies that continually generated new deals all over the world, some of which other lawyers at the firm hoped to acquire or had acquired subject to conflicts checks. It is not always easy for a lawyer to hold on to a prospective representation during the weeks that it may take to clear conflicts, so there was always pressure to move the process faster than possible, and negative responses naturally provoked disappointment. And the daily conflicts inquiries took up an inordinate amount of time.

The two other arbitrators on my panel were distinguished specialists, and they worked solo in order to avoid the conflicts issues that had to be addressed at law firms. They did not have to clear conflicts with respect to any matters other than their own. Also, there is little advantage to serving as an arbitrator from within a law firm because an arbitrator generally can not delegate any part of the work to other legal professionals at the firm. For these reasons, I decided to go back to working on my own.

The Shanghai *ayi* complained repeatedly about her long and tiring commute to my apartment. When I left the law firm, she began a campaign to get me to move house to Hongkou District, near her. Hongkou is rather different from tree-canopied Julu Road, scrappier, busier, both newer and older, the populace virtually 100% Chinese. It was getting gentrified, and I agreed to look at newly built apartments there. No longer needing to be near Nanjing West Road, I saw this as an opportunity to save money and to immerse myself in Chinese language and life in a way that was more difficult in the beautiful apartment on Julu Road or the sumptuous place in the China World Apartments in Beijing. In those places, many Chinese spoke fluent English, and there were considerable numbers of Westerners.

Fredric was visiting when the new abode was under discussion, and he accompanied me and the Shanghai *ayi* to inspect the place that I liked the best. He recalled with great relish the doorman who drew himself up and beamed with pride as he promoted the international quality of his building:

Zai sanshi ceng, you liangwei agentingren [There are two Argentines on the 30th floor]!

In fact, I never saw them or a single other *laowai* in the entire complex.

This apartment was largely unfurnished and would require numerous purchases at IKEA, eating up the savings in rent for at least two years, but the Shanghai *ayi* pronounced herself very clever for suggesting this move. Fredric was as taken with her as I, and we agreed that she had shown unerring judgment, so I made the move. The best place in the apartment was the seat built into the large, projecting casement window in the study which had a view of Hongkou and across the Huangpu River to Pudong and its garish towers. Below, not twenty feet across a narrow alley, there was a fascinating little old quarter. The Expressionist lines of its roofs and balconies and the endlessly changing array of added-on floors, walls, rooms, dormer windows, terraces, rooftop gardens were entrancing.

Once, I sighed to Mr. Z. that I would miss the trees of Julu Road and Xiangyang Park. Quickly erasing the concerned look on his face and smiling broadly, he observed:

["In no time at all, you'll see, Mr. Rothman, the park here will be filled with plants and trees and flowers".]

I took that remark as typical Chinese positivism, especially since there was no park nearby at all, only a barren patch of dirt. But the following year, after a long stay in the US, I visited the place with him. Lo and behold, it not only looked like a park but had become a magnificent, completely mature one. "How on earth did they ever do that", I asked myself. "Full blown, like Athena from the head of Zeus."

The Shanghai *ayi* had always seemed to be at the Julu Road apartment every day, but she was present literally all day, every day, at the apartment in Hongkou. It took her at most five minutes to walk there from the utter penury of her street. Even though she had nothing to do most of the time, it was not hard to understand why she preferred my place to her own. Not only was hers incredibly cramped, but her TV set looked like the first one ever sold, and she had no heat and no air conditioning.

I did not mind her being around. Within the narrow limits of her frame of reference, she was good enough company. So on days when I worked at home, the Shanghai *ayi* watched her soap operas or cooked or puttered or ran errands, and in free moments, I would come out of the study and pass the time of day with her. Sometimes, we went out to eat egg tarts or buy delicacies-pistachios, Ethiopian coffee, chocolate, or to grab a meal at a local restaurant, often joined by Mr. Z.

Coincidentally, Hongkou was the district where most Jews who fled to Shanghai found refuge, from Czarist pogroms, the Bolshevik Revolution, and Nazi death camps. For the most part, they were extremely poor, distinct from the wealthy caste of Iraqi and other Jews who had gone to Shanghai in the wake of the Opium Wars and helped build Shanghai's banking and other industries.

I made a great point of recounting to the Shanghai *ayi* and Mr. Z. the Jewish history of Hongkou. They knew only that there were two former synagogues in the district and had no idea about the Jews who had once used them, except, as Chinese are wont to say about Jews, at least to Jews, that ["[t]hey are very intelligent."] They had had no clue why the Jews had gone there in the first place or why they left. And other than me, they had never met a Jew. My voice sometimes shook as I explained that Shanghai was the only place open to those Jews, that as poor and crowded as Hongkou was, the Chinese never objected to having the Jews squeeze in with them.

I sometimes thought about the factors that caused the different circumstances of the Beijing and Shanghai *ayi*s. One was their personalities. Beijing *Ayi* was much more ambitious and energetic. Another was their age. When the Cultural Revolution began, Beijing *Ayi* was in her 20s and a member of a *danwei* [work unit] in Beijing, which allowed her to stay there and to get a modicum of an education, while the Shanghai *ayi*, in her teens and jobless, "went down", according to her, or more likely was "sent down", to the countryside "to learn from the peasants", digging ditches, milking cows, plowing fields, picking crops, and gathering manure.

The Shanghai *ayi* claimed that she became the *duizhang* [team head] of her *shengchan dui* [production team].[6] She would tell that she liked it so much in the boondocks that she stayed there 20 years. Although I never expressed any doubt to her, such a long sojourn in the countryside, really internal exile, was rare unless one married and settled down there or was serving a sentence for a serious crime. Also, the gung-ho approach that her story implied did not fit with the lassitude that now at least was the Shanghai *ayi*'s most prominent characteristic. Then again, disappointed expectations of some sort could have taken over. Millions of Chinese got caught up in the chaos that Mao and the Gang of Four stirred up only to be left with nothing to show for it in the end, not membership in the Communist Party or the Communist Youth League, not even an education. She never so much as mentioned the Party or the Youth League, although from the good times that she described in rural Jiangxi Province, she should have been glad, like Beijing *Ayi*, to volunteer that she was a member of either organization, had she been a member. Yet if she wasn't a member, it was hard to see why she would not have felt badly taken advantage of.

So, there was something odd about the Shanghai *ayi*'s nostalgia for her days in the countryside. On holidays, she would regale me with stories about members of her old production team showering visits and gifts on her and Mr. Z., although I never met any of these people or saw any of the gifts. Actually, she never said how Mr. Z. fitted into that group or where she and Mr. Z. met. In fact, no matter how many conversations we had, I never learned a shred more information about her family or friends other than Mr. and Mrs. L., and the tutor and his wife, and I knew next to nothing in the end about any of them other than that they all seemed like very nice people.

---

6 See footnote 3.

chapter eleven

In October 2008, I was working part-time in San Francisco and part-time in Shanghai. The crash of global financial markets that had begun with the collapse of Lehman Brothers in September was escalating, each day more violently. The BBC was running programs such as "Capitalism: A Tiger With Gaping Wounds." There was little business to be done anywhere, most of my friends were away from Shanghai, but I had last been in China in May, and that seemed so long. With the Beijing Olympics crowds gone, I decided to go back, more for personal interest than anything else. My best foreign friend in Shanghai, "U.", a lawyer colleague in past deals, had emailed to me for months clamoring for me to go back, and if nothing else, we always had a great time together. I also had something that I very much wanted to ask her in person.

As departure time, October 4, neared, amidst the market crash, the tumult of the Obama-McCain presidential race, and a prolonged and still unresolved misunderstanding between Fredric and me, I became uncharacteristically nervous about leaving the US. The trip began inauspiciously, with common travel mishaps, the worst of which was that, after arriving at the business class lounge at SFO, I discovered that I had brought no credit cards, very little cash, and no ID other than my passport, and no medical insurance card.

Even if something urgent were happening in Shanghai, it would have been foolhardy to leave in such disarray. But I never was one to turn back from a journey. As my final semester at Yale began, three friends and I cooked up a post-graduation travel odyssey to begin the day after graduation exercises. We had no idea of the itinerary we would take, but we grabbed up student charter tickets to Istanbul, with Bamiyan in Afghanistan the main destination. We slowly filled in some details, but the whole thing was deliberately vague, the way my parents traveled with our family when I was a kid. The only difference was that my folks liked to stay in palaces, and we would be going native, hotels for a dollar or less per night, travel mostly by local buses, total budget of USD 600 for four months including airfare. Even before the trip began, two of the group dropped out, including the one who spoke Farsi and Dari; the third gave up two weeks in, at the Iran-Afghanistan border. I went on by myself, determined to see everything that I could from Istanbul to the Vale of Kashmir. In the 1990s and 2000s, I had traveled all over China, by myself and with Fredric, to the remotest places, without serious incident. Shanghai was nothing like Xishuangbanna and the Upper Mekong, not to mention Afghanistan, and although I did not have the extensive network that I had in Beijing, I did have cash, a bank account, an apartment, some friends, and the Shanghai *ayi* and her family.

I had some health issues, my bad back and sciatica which had caused me to gain weight, sinus problems since childhood that led to respiratory illnesses, and carpal tunnel syndrome in my left hand and forearm. My main ailment was insomnia. Starting when I was 17, through years of cramming for exams, working on Wall Street, and then on international matters, my insomnia became more and more serious, and I needed to take prescription sleeping medicine most nights in order to sleep.

For the first week back in Shanghai, I had planned a few dinners with friends visiting from the US and Europe, at Laris on the Bund and T8 in Xintiandi, two of the standard *laowai* hangouts. And meetings with an existing client and a prospective one about new projects, an industrial joint venture in one of Shanghai's special investment zones, and a large commercial lease and buildout near the Bund. But these projects were merely preliminary; no one seemed inclined to commit to anything at that moment with global markets unable to find a bottom.

Fearful as I was of not sleeping, it was more than odd that I hardly noticed for the first week or ten days back in Shanghai that I was not sleeping at all. Night after night, I remained awake, surfing the Web, reading and writing torrents of emails, often just looking out at the darkened old district, the few lights on Sichuan North Road, and, through mist and murk, the distant towers of the international financial district and Pudong. As the days passed, I felt more and more exhausted. I had little appetite, but the Shanghai *ayi*'s soups always went down easily, and after I had some of that, I would feel a surge of energy.

Not one of my Chinese or expat friends turned out to be in Shanghai, not even "U." who had promised to be there long before I arrived, so I took outings, in the nearby old quarter, on the new light rail lines that seemed to go from nothing a year before to a complete network that criss-crossed the city, and with the Shanghai *ayi* and Mr. Z. to their Buddhist temple which was of the "patriotic" or state-controlled variety. I was in very good spirits, ebullient at times, even though it seemed as though sleeplessness had become a permanent condition. I had never gone for more than two nights without sleeping at all, but now I sometimes wondered if I would be like the Vietnamese woman who claimed in an interview in the 1990s that she had not slept since 1965 and had lived in a sort of mental penumbra for decades.

chapter twelve

On Tuesday morning, October 21, 2008, I returned from a rejuvenating walk in the park with Mr. Z. to find the apartment trashed. Haggard from a totally unprecedented bout of 16 days of nearly complete insomnia, but emotionally high from the walk and the golden weather, it took a few seconds for me to comprehend what had happened. Books, DVDs, CDs, music scores, clothes had been strewn everywhere, files and papers from eight years of work and stacks of newspapers flung about wildly, incense ashes scattered over every surface.

I felt something like panic, but it was fear, not a panic attack. Butterflies roiled my stomach as I examined the front door, undamaged, the lock, not forced or tampered with, the same with the door to the terrace and the one from the kitchen to the back stairs. No one answered at the Shanghai *ayi*'s apartment, her cell phone likewise. My instinct was to flee. I raced around the apartment trying to think of the most important things that I could take with me in a small roll-on and a computer bag.

The cash drawer in the bedroom was unlocked as usual, 50,000 *renminbi* and USD 5,000-6,000, all there. I had withdrawn the *renminbi* to pay the next three months' rent and salary for the Shanghai *ayi* and household expenses and brought the dollars from the US in recent trips but had forgotten to deposit them. I threw the money into my computer bag along with some of my father's cuff links, one pair with gold Austria-Hungary *kronen* bearing the image of Emperor Franz Josef I and another of apple-green jade.

Next, the study. Which client files to take? Hopeless. "I have almost all the important stuff on my laptop," I said to myself. My CDs, my DVDs! A very large, expensive collection, all brought from the US over the years. How could I say which were indispensable? I simply took the ones that peeked out from the mess. Music scores, more expensive, hopelessly big and heavy, would have to stay. I went back to the bedroom, grabbed some clothes, threw everything in the foyer near the front door, then stuffed things inside the roll-on and computer bag. Now that I could run if I had to, I began to calm down.

More than an hour passed. The Shanghai *ayi*, Mr. Z., "YY", none of them answered their phones. I pushed some papers off a chair in the living room and sat down: "Why should I flee? From what to what? Why spend the money on a hotel room and to change my plane reservation?" Then, I said out loud: "This is where Jews came to get away from danger. Am I going to be *the* first Jew *ever* to *flee* Hongkou?"

I began pacing, as if that would produce better mental clarity, nudging aside things in the way with my feet, bending carefully to pick up others. I tried desperately to figure out who had done this and why. As I looked around, I realized that my office equipment, running machine, furniture, the elegant stereo, were untouched. The kitchen was clean, a big pot of my favorite meat ball soup on the counter. Did someone ransack the place for sensitive papers? Again, I tried the Shanghai *ayi*; no answer. My back pain and sciatica were killing me by now.

A few more hours passed. I still had no clues, but the sense of imminent danger began to recede. I was in the kitchen getting some water when the Shanghai *ayi* turned her key in the lock. My first feeling was relief at the thought that she might have some simple explanation, though objectively, even the most radical spring cleaning would not have created such a mess.

I caught sight of her from behind the kitchen door as she gingerly stuck her head around the corner between the foyer and the living room. Her face expressed no surprise at the scene in front of her. She took a few more steps into the living room then turned back into the foyer. On tiptoes, I went into the living room, making a wide berth away from her so as not to shock her unduly, and watched for a minute as she bent to examine the roll-on and computer bag. She turned toward the living room, then we were *vis-à-vis*, about fifteen feet apart. Extending my left arm toward the mess in the living room, taking a deep breath, I asked as calmly as possible:

Ayi, shei dao luanle? Fashengle shenma shi [Ayi, who created such chaos here? What happened]?

She looked right at me but not into my eyes, her head tilted, lips curled ever so slightly as if to smile; a second later, without saying a word, she bolted.

["It was you"!] I shouted after her. She turned her head but said nothing as she turned back, struggled for a moment to open the front door, then broke into a run, making for the stairway. A surge of electric energy shot through me, making me forget my aches and pains. I dashed out and caught up with her in the landing, grabbed her left arm, tore the keys from her right hand.

Nide xinli you shenma gui [What demons are there in your heart]? I said, in a clenched tone. *Ni weishenma zheyang zuole* [Why did you do it]?

She still said nothing, looking at me with veiled eyes.

["Did you do this?"]

No answer.

["Did you do this? Why?"]

Silence. Then, with a contemptuous smirk on her face, she went limp. I shook her arm, she yanked her head away violently, I shook her arm again, she only went more limp, now like a cloth doll. I was so enraged that I could have thrown her down the ten flights of stairs. I fixed on the pathetically thin gold chain with a minuscule, heart-shaped charm that she always wore and wanted to rip it off and shove it down her throat. But I stopped myself. "Mr. Z. must have saved for five years to buy her that," I thought later, thankful then that I had not let my rage go that far. I loosened my grip on her arm, and she tore away and raced down the stairs. I screamed after her, at the top of my lungs:

Jiang Qing di er; Jiang Qing di er; Jiang Qing di er; Jiang Qing di er [Jiang Qing the Second], my voice careening off the concrete walls and floors of the stairwell.

Breathless, I staggered inside and slammed the door. I hardly noticed that my affection for the Shanghai *ayi* had turned into a hatred that I had never felt. I went to the kitchen sink to splash water on my face. On the counter was the Shanghai *ayi*'s brilliantly patterned apron. I took a cleaver to it, cutting my right index finger in the process. I barely paid attention to the blood that spurted out, wrapped a paper towel around the cut, and went through the apartment room by room, pushing things into corners, all the while cursing under my breath and out loud in Chinese and English. But other than the Shanghai *ayi*, I was at a loss as to whom to curse, much less why.

Suddenly, I noticed something that stopped me cold. Years before, I had carelessly brought to China *The Tiananmen Papers* edited by Andrew Nathan and Perry Link. The most seditious book that one could possess in China, it reproduces key documents concerning the Chinese leadership's decisions and actions ordering the 1989 massacre and brutal imprisonment of thousands of pro-democracy protesters in Tiananmen Square and additional thousands of protesters in dozens of cities all over China, the memory of which still terrifies the regime more than any other and which it does everything in its power to eradicate. But I never had worried about bringing the book through

Chinese customs. In all of my trips in and out of China, no one had once opened a single piece of my luggage. Now the book scared the life out of me.

"What if the police come here," I moaned as I ripped and pulled at it and tore up pages. I grabbed some sutras that I had picked up during the previous week's visit to the Shanghai *ayi*'s "patriotic" Buddhist temple and shredded them. "'Patriotic temple', my ass. Dogshit puppet temple," I yelled as I mixed the fragments of the book with pieces of the sutras.

Whirling around like a dervish, I threw pile after pile of torn and soiled papers on to the terrace. Some of them floated down to the street, including some from *The Tiananmen Papers*. I realized my stupidity: many Shanghainese read English. But I told myself, "Maybe they'll just sweep it up with the rest of the muck down there. They also walk past children hit by a car, dying in the road. Fearful people, country built on fear." Indeed, no one seemed to even glance at the papers that were carpeting the street, much less pick them up.

Now it was raining heavily. The Indian Summer of the walk in the park with Mr. Z. was over. I went inside, turned on the heat, and as I dried off, wrote a denunciation in Chinese of the Shanghai *ayi* which I placed on the breakfast table. I went to the kitchen and ladled out a bowl of the meat ball soup. "No. I won't take a mouthful of her food," I said out loud as I slammed the bowl down on the breakfast table, slopping over some of the soup. I was only thirsty anyway and drank a glass of water, then went back to sorting things to concentrate the more important items in the center of the Xinjiang carpet in the living room. Maybe it would be possible to have them shipped to San Francisco.

I must have grasped dimly that this was the beginning of the end of my China sojourns. I noticed a CD set, *Die Götterdämmerung* (*The Twilight of the Gods*). I had a duplicate, so I decided to leave it behind. I loved Wagner's music but hated his virulent anti-Semitism and the Nazis' reverence for him. So I scribbled "Down with tyranny" and "Down with Hitler" on the labels of the discs as I played at the highest conceivable volume the Ride of the Valkyries, then the Immolation Scene. I now felt better, as if Birgit Nilsson's titanic high notes had defied the evil that had visited my apartment.

I decided to stay put, for now. As night fell, I thought to call the US Consulate. I had never been there and had never met anyone with the Consulate. A duty officer answered the phone. I told him what had happened. He made some sympathetic remarks but offered no help or suggestions:

"Are you in danger?"

"I guess so."

"Did you call the police?"

"No. Who would do that in China?"

"Uh, I see your point. I'll give you my phone number, but there's little we can do."

I wrote his name and phone number on a Post-it which I stuck on the refrigerator door. In my distress, had I forgotten to tell him that the US Ambassador and his wife were my friends? Had I remembered to mention that would it have made a difference? Had I been able to get to the Post-it a few days later, would that have made a difference?

The telephone rang. I jumped less from surprise than a hope that it was Mr. Z. or "YY" who now might explain everything. But it was "Q.":

"*Ayi* told me there is some problem."

I had not seen or spoken with "Q." since his blurt-out at dinner the previous May. It is difficult to know what I thought about him at that moment. We had exchanged emails before I returned to Shanghai. Some concerned a plan that he mentioned for the first time in August - to apply to

Columbia Law School - and his request for a letter of recommendation, in some of them he urged me to return to Shanghai. A few were fanciful exchanges after I got back to Shanghai.

Could I have forgotten, disarmed by a friendly sounding voice? Did I think that "Q." in the end might not have gone through with the bribe? Did I assume that because "Q." said that he wanted to go to law school in the US and sought my recommendation that he had nothing to hide? At any rate, I told him what had happened:

"I don't know what is going on; the place was trashed while I was out, and *Ayi* must have done it. No one else had a key, no sign that someone broke in. She dashed out of here like a thief and wouldn't speak to me. Not a single word. I need to get some soup; I won't eat her stuff. I wouldn't be surprised if she threw rat poison into it. Let's talk tomorrow."

I hung up the phone, looked around for a few more items, put on a rain slicker and grabbed an umbrella. Just as I was leaving, "Q." arrived with takeout food. I was surprised that he came over, but also glad not to have to go out, and grateful for his thoughtfulness.

"How did you get here so fast?" I asked. "Q." didn't answer, and before I could ask why he had come, he changed the subject. Pointing at the soup bowl and the spilled soup, he said: "Heh, heh. You *really* don't like her food anymore." I thanked him for the take-out. The dishes were unusually delicious, but hunger quickly vanished, and I ate only a few bites. "Q." ate nothing, saying that he had just had dinner.

"How is your mother? Did she come to Shanghai with you?" I asked. He had emailed that he was vacationing with her in Suzhou. "What about Suzhou, beautiful as always?"

He shrugged his shoulders. As he looked around the living room, he said:

"I can't imagine *Ayi* doing such a thing."

"Tell me exactly, what did *Ayi* say to you, the first thing out of her mouth when she called you."

"Q." waved his hand in an inconclusive way and responded: "I don't know."

"Did she say why she called you?"

It wasn't all that surprising that the Shanghai *ayi* would try to contact "Q." since they had met when he used to come to my place to work for me. But how did she have his telephone number?

"Have you spoken with her recently, before her call today?"

"Q." kept answering with shrugs. I could get nothing out of him. "One local protecting another," I thought.

I asked: "What are you going to tell *Ayi* now?"

"What do you want me to tell her? Do you want her to come back to clean the place up?"

"I don't know. I don't know what to think. Why did she do it? If she didn't do it, why didn't she say that she didn't, why did she flee? Does she know who did it? Ask her those things. Then I can decide whether she comes back here."

Then I added: "What about the screen? Did you ask your father whether his company can ship it to San Francisco for me?"

"Q." said that his father was too busy for him to ask right now. After a few more minutes' small talk, he left.

chapter thirteen

I felt more wretched than ever. The excitement, however unpleasant, the relief, from recounting what had happened, the hope, that "Q." might shed light on the situation, all drained away and left me perplexed and sad. I had no idea what to do next and shuffled aimlessly around the apartment. Little by little, though, the sight of familiar things that I had acquired in China and the thoughts that they evoked were comforting.

The tangkas

My most prized possessions from China were the Tibetan *tangkas* that covered all of the available wall space in the apartment. I often gazed at their beauty and sought their calm spirituality. Fredric and I had bought many in Panjiayuan, a flea market in Beijing. Gorgeous arrays of images and colors, Buddhas and boddhisatvas, in gold, silver, copper presiding over bejeweled and verdant paradises.

Buddhism reached its full flower in China during the Tang Dynasty (618-907). The Tang and the role of Buddhism in Chinese history were two of Arthur Wright's specializations. His courses introduced Buddhist art as well as the tenets of Buddhism, and that is how I discovered the great Chinese Buddhist cave temples, Dunhuang, Longmen, Yungang, Dazu. The very names thrilled me, and I developed an intense longing to see them. The friends with whom I planned a post-graduation odyssey in 1970 also were interested in Chinese Buddhism, but as Americans, we could not travel to China. However, the Chinese cave temples were modeled on those at Bamiyan, a major Buddhist center of the ancient Kingdom of Gandhara in the Hindu Kush mountains of present-day Afghanistan. Situated astride the India-China Silk Road, Gandhara was a fantastic cultural melting pot with influences ranging from Indian to Greek, the latter the legacy of Alexander the Great who passed through on his way to the Indus River. So that is why Bamiyan, with its Colossal Buddhas, became our principal destination, or rather my destination in the end.

As appealing as Buddhism and Buddhist art were, it was as an operatic tenor that I first turned to the Buddha for spiritual help, and that created an intimate and indelible association in my mind between opera and Buddhism that the *tangkas* brought to mind.

In the mid-1980s, the initial rush of China work subsided as China exhausted its limited capacity to absorb foreign investment. I decided to throw myself into opera singing once again, virtually full time. It didn't matter that an international career no longer was feasible. I had to prove to myself that I could master and perform leading tenor roles at a professional level, and this required many hours per day of voice, coaching, and acting lessons and learning music. Other than a few performances in the late 1960s as the tenor lead in Benjamin Britten's *Curlew River*, a "church parable", and a few performances as Peter Pan in eighth grade, I had never been in a staged production, or had to sing solo on stage for more than a few minutes, or had to sing a note above the staff.[7] It was daunting to say the least to approach as my first and second leading roles, within a few months of each other, the Prince in Rossini's *La Cenerentola* and Belmonte in Mozart's *The Abduction from the Seraglio*, and in between, the tenor soloist in Haydn's *Stabat Mater*, all with orchestra, all extremely long, high-lying parts, with endless high B flats, Bs, and Cs, even a C sharp.

Though satisfying in the end, these early performances gave me terrible stage fright, sometimes to the point of nausea. I didn't so much go out on stage as get peeled off the backstage walls and pushed onstage. Before solos in college and high school choir concerts, my friends used to joke that the greener my pallor beforehand the better I sang, but the far greater exposure and technical demands of opera brought stage fright to an extreme level. Insecurity in my high range, the tenor's "money notes", was the root of the problem; nothing is more fear-inducing for a singer than to not be sure what is going to happen when he or she goes for a high note.

In 1986, the Spanish tenor Alfredo Kraus came to the San Francisco Opera for the first of three seasons. I had long admired him above all other lyric tenors for his effortless and flawless high range. More than 40 years into a huge career, with hundreds of recordings to his credit, he showed no sign of letting up and was in demand in every major opera house in the world. As with Maestro Weede, his vocal longevity was a crucial indication of the quality of his technique. I had to seize the possibility of singing for him and get whatever technical advice he could give me, in whatever minutes he could spare. After pulling every string and deploying every stratagem I could think of, I managed to meet him and persuade him to hear me:

"Mr. Rothman, your high notes are uneven. Some of them would never project in a large house."

---

7 That is, high G and above.

I was a bit crestfallen that he went right to that issue. I had worked so hard on that part of my voice, but neither was I surprised since that was the main reason I wanted his help. Then he said:

"But you have an exceptional instrument, and I will help you. Of course, you must understand that my free time is always very limited."

I was elated. This was far beyond anything I had dreamed of. As it turned out, he was incredibly generous with his time, and a very effective teacher. Toward the end of the season, he suggested that I send him cassette tapes which he would critique by letter.

Before I would be able to see him again, my toughest performing situation loomed, in which my grasp of what I had learned from him would be tested to the maximum. By itself, the music was not especially challenging, a single aria in an operatic pageant. But it was the centerpiece of the entire show and required an heroic sound, and the setting was a vast outdoor stage in a redwood forest in Sonoma County, the summer retreat of the Bohemian Club. With no acoustical shell and no natural feedback to the singer, it was the sort of space and the sort of music that can make one push the voice with sheer muscle power, which can lead to a strangled, unresonant sound at best and complete vocal paralysis at worst. Indeed, more than one singer who performed this piece came to grief somewhere in the middle, reduced to mouthing the words, yet the audience is waiting for a final, crescendoing, stentorian high note that is supposed to be held as long as humanly possible.

The other conditions could not have been worse. The air there in July is dry as a bone, filled with pollen, dust, and wood smoke, perilous for sinuses like mine. Forty-five minutes before dusk, my character, a wood sprite, climbs a ladder unobserved into a hollowed-out, spider-infested redwood tree that is part of the stage. When the sky is completely dark, the show begins. Twenty minutes into the performance, the stage goes pitch black, and I am to slither out and around a tiny bark door, a single, blinding spot suddenly shining on me, the sole character on stage, and in the same movement, without getting my costume caught, close the door and come to rest on a tiny platform, without falling head first to the forest floor twelve feet below. And then sing to an invisible audience of several thousand assembled across a pond, over a large orchestra, the conductor invisible except for his white-gloved hand. There was only one rehearsal on stage with the orchestra, in daylight, on the afternoon of the performance, and no rehearsal in costume, which made it impossible to get accustomed to the staging and the acoustics.

As the performance approached, a sense of frozen, abject hopelessness set in at the merest thought of it. Exactly two weeks before the appointed date, I awoke in a cold sweat and said to Fredric: "I'm not going to get through this thing alive. I'll get stuck on the bark door, or I am going to plunge right off that platform. My throat is going to close up, my sinuses will kill me, a bug will fly into my mouth, my voice will crack on the high note, or I won't get that far."

Casting about for a way to calm myself, I remembered some meditation tapes and books from a Tibetan Buddhist institute that I had bought a few years before but had never used. The first few days of trying to learn the breathing exercises brought no improvement at all in my state of mind, and as I contemplated an impending disaster, I realized that I deserved no mercy for turning so opportunistically and belatedly to meditation. The Buddha teaches that you must not do these things with an ulterior, worldly purpose, and meditation practice is not learned overnight. But since I could think of no other salvation, I kept at it. To my great surprise, by the fourth or fifth day, I felt a distinct lightening of my mood, so I re-doubled my efforts. It became clear to me that the breathing used for this school of meditation was basically the same as the breathing that Maestro Kraus propounded. The goals were different, but the physical concept the same.

The day of the performance arrived. The afternoon rehearsal went tenuously but passably, well enough to sustain a guarded hope. Whenever possible, I found some spot in which to do the breathing exercises and to inhale steam.

Showtime! Completely calm, I climbed the ladder, crouched inside the tree, breathed as well as I could in that space. Phew. The spiders and cobwebs were gone, thanks to my good friend, the costume master, who had cleaned them out. A good omen, and singers love good omens. At the downbeat for my number, I glided out the bark door, came to rest, prepared my stance, chest riding comfortably high, back ribs expanded and working gently, like a bellows, throat relaxed and elastic. I smiled at the spotlight, it seemed the sun, raised my arms in greeting, and my whole body sang:

Beauty and strength and peace,

they are yours, they shall never cease...

One's best singing demands total concentration, and in that moment my voice responded directly to my musical and dramatic mind without reference to anything else, least of all fear or hesitation. I received a joyous ovation, and I treasure the recording that I was given later. I knew that I had made major progress when Señora Kraus, the fierce guardian of the Maestro's schedule, told me a few months later when they returned to San Francisco: "We really liked your last tape." So she listened to them as well. The best compliment of all. The selections on that tape included this piece and several with many high Bs and Cs, the Maestro's calling cards. No evaluation could have been more important to me. I started going to classes and retreats at the Tibetan institute, and I never again performed anything without doing meditation and breathing exercises beforehand.

Now, amidst the mess of what my friends jokingly called my "Shanghai mini-palace," the memory of that experience gave me much needed courage. I thought about the marvelous retreat that I had attended just a few weeks earlier, how calm and complete the meditation practice made me feel. I looked around at the *tangkas* and breathed deeply, the first full breaths that I had taken since I returned to the apartment that morning. Then, I stood in front of each one, scrutinizing it, pondering it, seeking its counsel. A prayer came to my lips, despite myself in Chinese: *Amituofu, pusa, baohu* [Amitabha, boddhisatvas, protect me]. I realized that I was bidding them farewell, possibly forever. Near tears, I took them off their hooks, one by one, and turned them to face the wall. I did not want these images to look upon the ugly state of affairs in the apartment.

The Mao Zedong-Lin Biao placard

*O*n a lovely day in May, 2007, I was walking with Mr. Z. and the Shanghai *ayi* on Wenhua [Culture] Street, off Sichuan North Road, where some noted literary figures such as Lu Xun had lived in the 1920s and 30s. At one of the curio stalls, I saw a standing, ceramic placard, about 12 inches high, that depicted Chairman Mao and his one-time designated heir, Lin Biao, complete with Cultural Revolutionary slogans. Mao and Lin are standing at a reviewing stand, Lin dutifully clutching a copy of Mao's *Little*

Red Book. Inscribed just below the images of Mao and Lin: ["Chairman Mao and his intimate comrade-in-arms, Comrade Lin Biao, inspect the great army of the Cultural Revolution."] Then: ["Read Chairman Mao's books. Listen to Chairman Mao's words. Carry out work according to the instructions of Chairman Mao."] On the back of the placard: ["Chairman Mao's latest instruction: 'Historical experience is worth paying attention to. One line, one point of view must frequently be taught, repeatedly taught. Merely teaching a small minority of the people is not good, the broad, revolutionary masses also must be taught.'"] One of those theories of Mao that is both insipid and profound.

I felt the breath of history, and I had to buy the placard, to go with my other Cultural Revolution kitsch, a plate of similar design and a ceramic set of Mr. and Mrs. Mao in their easy chairs, sipping tea and discussing Confucius' *Analects*. I knew at one glance that the placard was genuine, but I deferred to Mr. Z.:

Shi zhen dongxi, Z. xiansheng [Is it real, Mr. Z.]?

Mr. Z. inspected the thing with tremendous attention to detail.

Shide. Shi zhen dongxi, Luo xiansheng [It is. It's real, Mr. Rothman].

The price had to be trivial, but it had become second nature to me to bargain for just about anything in China. I hesitated to involve Mr. Z. and already felt a bit awkward about having shown interest in the thing. Lin Biao clawed his way to the top during the Cultural Revolution which was one issue since I had no idea how Mr. Z. fared then. The other issue was that Chinese are taught that Lin Biao was the worst traitor in Chinese Communist history, to the extent that he is mentioned at all. In 1971, Mao caught his "intimate comrade-in-arms Comrade Lin Biao" plotting a coup. With his nefarious wife, Ye Qun, the bosom friend of Jiang Qing, Lin fled in his passenger jet, but Chinese fighter planes shot it down over Mongolia, making Lin the last of a long line of rivals of Mao to bite the dust.

Since Mr. Z. continued to look at the placard, picking it up and turning it around and upside down, I could see that he was not uncomfortable either on account of the banned memory of Lin Biao or how he may have been treated back then. So, despite the fact that I enjoyed haggling with Chinese merchants, bantering with them, walking away as many times as necessary, I felt that I had to turn the matter over to Mr. Z. The money was too little to worry about, and I did not want to risk offending him by infringing on his expertise or by carrying on in a way that this soft-spoken man might find unseemly. I drew Mr. Z. away from the stall and asked him whether he would mind negotiating for me. Mr. Z. smiled broadly, released a large amount of air through his mouth, took another breath, then said with great seriousness:

Wo qu wenyiwen [I'll go inquire]. *Nimen waiguo ren, tamen hui pian nimen* [They're likely to cheat you foreigners].

Mr. Z. knocked the price down by a few *renminbi* and pronounced that an excellent deal. Given the alacrity with which the stall owner accepted Mr. Z.'s bid, I knew that I could have gotten it for a third less, and Fredric, the best bargainer I've ever seen in China, could have gotten it for half, but I could not ask Mr. Z. to continue the negotiation or take over myself, so I accepted with gratitude:

Ni hen hui tanjia huanjia, Z. xiansheng [You are really a great bargainer, Mr. Z.]!

I treated Mr. Z. and the Shanghai *ayi* to a celebratory tea at a nearby shop where Mr. Z. continued on this theme:

["These shop owners, they don't have any morals. They'll cheat anyone who doesn't know better. Not just you foreigners, also tourists from the countryside. But of course they know that you can pay much more."]

It always made me bristle when Chinese took this sort of patronizing, didactic attitude, as if I had no eyes and ears, no common sense, no normal brain capacity, no experience in China. It rankled especially when I knew a subject better than they, but I held back from expressing any annoyance to Mr. Z. He meant well.

Now, the placard rested on top of a pile of clothes on the Xinjiang carpet. Despite everything, the memory of that purchase made me smile.

The camphorwood screen

On a hot, lazy afternoon in Beijing, in the Summer of 2004, Beijing *Ayi* trooped into my apartment with her stepson in tow. I had told her that I wanted to buy Chinese furniture, and he had located a warehouse in a remote district of the city that had just put on sale a trove of items which, according to the stepson, had been seized for non-payment of taxes. It would not have surprised me if this property in fact were the product of some anti-corruption campaign.

The contents of the place were dazzling. The fifth floor held things of jade and ivory and gold, jewelry, implements, furniture, some adorned with precious stones the likes of which I had only seen in museums or royal palaces. With one glance, I knew that these were so far beyond my means that it would hurt to ask the prices, so I focused on the third and fourth floors which held mostly lacquered furniture and porcelain. We came across a beautifully carved camphorwood screen whose fragrance was apparent even in that vast, musty space. I settled upon the screen. After Beijing *Ayi* and I dickered in tandem with the attendant for 30 or so minutes, the price still was too high, so we changed tactics and went off on a tangent, expressing the suspicion that the management had sprayed the screen with camphor oil, then, that it was carved by machine, not hand. The attendant refuted these points to our satisfaction, and Beijing *Ayi* clinched the deal with a final and decisive offer. The screen was boxed up and tied to the top of the stepson's car, and we returned in triumph to my apartment where the new treasure became the centerpiece of my living room. I moved it with me to Shanghai.

As I looked at the screen, now a sort of landmark in a debris field, its sight and smell, and its elegantly carved images of graceful women captured in mid-dance, transported me back to another happy time, an idyll with Fredric.

Shang you Tiantang,

Xia you Su Hang.

[Above there is Paradise,

Below there are Su(zhou) and Hang(zhou)].

Hangzhou was the capital of the Southern Song Dynasty (1127-1279) which represents for many the pinnacle of Chinese artistic achievement. It was unspoiled when Fredric and I went there for the first time, in 1994. Fabled gardens, magical West Lake, surrounded by astonishingly green hills with tea plantations where rare varieties were cultivated, where camphor trees imparted a magical aroma to the misty, humid night air. It was May, the rainy season, at first to us a disadvantage until we discovered that Chinese prize that season in Hangzhou, precisely because of the rain and mist and clouds. Soaked but happy, we sloshed around for days, visiting the many fabulous historic sights.

Fredric had long since taught me the benefit, if not quite his love, of jogging; every morning we ran around West Lake just after dawn. The shifting views in the morning mist were intoxicating. In pavilions along the shore, middle-aged and elderly couples danced to Western ballroom music played from boom boxes. During the Cultural Revolution, this type of dancing was banned and severely punished. One incident that involved such dancing was notorious in all of China.

In 1963, with Mao Zedong sidelined because of his catastrophic Great Leap Forward (1958-62)[8], and with Liu Shaoqi and more moderate leaders in control of the country, one of those few poignant gusts of slight political relaxation blew briefly in Communist China. An example of the mood was seen during the state visit to Indonesia by Liu and his wife, Wang Guangmei. They were photographed dancing at a ball in Jakarta given in their honor, Wang wearing pearls and a silk *qipao*. Not the attire of revolutionaries, definitely not the lumpy, shapeless military-style uniform worn by Jiang Qing, and most certainly not the behavior of revolutionaries.

Wang, out in public, at times given senior political assignments, glamorous, from a wealthy family, highly educated, incited a maniacal jealousy in Jiang Qing whose background could not have been more different. The daughter of an abused second wife of a small landlord who drove out mother and daughter, Jiang was a former itinerant vaudeville singer, then grade B movie actress in Shanghai in the 1930s. Her tawdry love affairs, the suicide of one of her lovers, her disastrous marriages were the subject of lurid articles in the Shanghai tabloids. She became a sort of marginal member of the Party, and when the scandals became unbearable for her, she made her way to Yan'an, Mao's redoubt in Shaanxi

---

8 See footnote 3.

Province in the Northwest during the civil war with Chiang Kai-shek and the Nationalists. She became Mao's mistress, and after he divorced wife number two, his wife. But because of her unsavory past, the other party leaders insisted that she be accorded no party rank to speak of and no public role.

In 1966, Mao staged a counter-coup and seized back power by launching his final mass movement, another devastating catastrophe, the Great Proletarian Cultural Revolution (1966-1976), and to do so, he literally unleashed Jiang Qing on his enemies and the nation.[9] Indeed, she testified at her trial, in 1980/81: ["I was Chairman Mao's dog. When he said 'bark' I barked. Whomever he said to bite, I bit."]

Jiang Qing proved indispensable in mobilizing an extreme left-wing faction with whose help Mao ousted Liu Shaoqi and his faction, now labeled "right-wing opportunists". She wasted no time in avenging past slights.

9 See footnote 2.

Liu and Wang were dragged to a platform in a Beijing sports arena, dunce caps on their heads, Wang forced to wear that same *qipao*, now slashed and mud-spattered, and an enormous necklace and earrings made out of ping pong balls to pay her back for those pearls. They were beaten in front of the crowd of 100,000. The photographs of that moment are horrifying. Liu died a terrible death in prison, Wang somehow survived her harsh incarceration.

By the early 1990s, ballroom dancing, characterized as morning exercise, had begun to be widely practiced. The disconnect between the Cultural Revolutionary era, what these Hangzhou dancers had witnessed and lived through, and the enchanting scene before us, created an intense, unforgettable feeling of historical dissonance. We felt a pang of sadness for these people and their lost youth and wanted to get closer to them.

In the midst of one of our jogs, we walked into a lakeside *ting* [pavilion] and sat down. Three elderly ladies came over and looked at us, at first timidly, then more boldly. They focused their attention on Fredric's prominent nose. A very handsome nose, but a Mediterranean one most unfamiliar to them. *Shenma guojia you bizi duoma dade ren* [What country has people with such big noses]? one asked another. When I interrupted their speculations with a pleasantry, they looked at me with even greater amazement because they could not imagine a *laowai* speaking Mandarin. Then they noticed that I have blue eyes which made them almost gasp. Murmuring to each other, they touched my face in turn, gently pressing each of their fingers on my cheeks, as if they were touching a rare, tame monkey.

It was the kind of experience that made us think that we were invulnerable in China. That feeling was only heightened by the journeys that we later made to very remote places, where we didn't see other Westerners for a week at a time, or at all. People always seemed to respect us for our admiration for and knowledge of their country. In all circumstances in which I had found myself over several decades of China work and travel, never had I encountered a situation where I could not deploy my Chinese language to solve whatever problems arose. Beyond all these factors, there was the clear Party policy that made violent incidents with *laowai* taboo.

chapter fourteen

The Hangzhou ballroom dancers, Liu Shaoqi and Wang Guangmei, the Mao-Lin Biao placard, the associations they evoked, swirled kaleidoscopically in my mind, until, suddenly, one memory, much more recent, brought those fantasies to an abrupt halt: "Ah, the criticism-struggle meeting!"

Actually, to describe that way the events of the previous Saturday had been a deliberate exaggeration. It was not a "criticism-struggle" meeting, such as the one inflicted on Liu Shaoqi and Wang Guangmei. No one used physical violence on me. It was more like a "criticism-education" meeting, a less severe type of Cultural Revolutionary kangaroo court where cadres and angry representatives of "the masses" merely harassed people verbally (though sometimes until the victim dropped dead) concerning some class background flaw or "counter-revolutionary" taste or point of view, or just to get even with someone in a private dispute.

"YY" called on the telephone:

["My mother is very concerned about you. We are coming over right now to hold a meeting."]

They must have been downstairs, or in the stairwell, for in the blink of an eye, they appeared at my door. The Shanghai *ayi* said gravely: ["We're worried that people will say that we have been remiss in taking care of you because you don't sleep. We will lose face."]

["Oh, is that all. I thought that it was something serious. Impossible. You can't be responsible for whether I sleep or not. Anyway, who told you that you are responsible for me at all? You help me with different things, and that is the basis of our friendship."]

She shrugged her shoulders, "YY" nodded his head in some direction, not all up and down and not all sideways either. Who could they possibly think they had to answer to concerning my welfare? The limitations of our legal and even our personal relationship appeared to be lost on them.

["Why are you not sleeping? We need to get to the bottom of this"], the Shanghai *ayi* said in the same low voice.

We went to the living room where "YY" placed two dining chairs opposite the easy chair in which I usually sat. I took my seat, and with the greatest solemnity, the Shanghai *ayi* motioned to "YY" to sit down, then she followed, and with a brittle *Kai hui* [Begin the meeting]! she formally commenced the proceeding.

["We must get to the bottom of your insomnia problem"], they said, almost in unison.

["My mother is so worried about you that she sometimes cries"], "YY" quickly added, but not with a very convincing tone or expression.

"Goodness," I thought. "The Chinese are so melodramatic!"

["When was the last time you slept?"] asked the Shanghai *ayi*.

I tried to remember, but I couldn't. ["I don't really know, but even though I have been feeling very tired lately, I feel surprisingly well. You know, *Ayi*, when I don't sleep, I complain to you constantly, get morose, hate to do anything at all. But I'm really fine, don't worry, please. I've been going out for walks, to take photos. Remember our little outings with Mr. Z.? Oh, and my visit with the opera singer and her husband in the old district?"]

At the last sentence, the Shanghai *ayi*'s face twisted itself into an ugly expression that stunned me, surprising and reminding me of something at the same time.

She changed the subject. ["You will soon die if you don't sleep, and anyway, you are losing all of your hair."]

I quickly touched my head to check and did not notice anything amiss.

["My mother and I and my father are so worried about you. We stay up all night talking about what to do"], "YY" interjected, in a flat tone.

["Wow, this is the first time that I heard that insomnia is a transmissible disease."]

They didn't laugh. So, I added quickly:

["Well, your mother did come over at 3am a few nights ago with her meatball soup, but I told her that she should not do that."]

So it went, for a seeming eternity. "YY" played the good cop, and the Shanghai *ayi* the bad cop. At one point, I found the situation so amusing that, laughing hysterically, I thought to mock the inquisitors of the Cultural Revolution who crammed cloths into the mouths of their victims to prevent them from saying anything that they did not want the crowd to hear. I grabbed a hand towel and stuffed it into my mouth.

["Now you can't force me to speak"], my voice muffled.

The Shanghai *ayi*'s face now was so ferocious looking that she would have scared me had I not known her so well. But I had no answers, no idea why my insomnia was so extreme.

The more lightly I took their concerns, the more tense they became. I was going to joke that the only thing missing was a dunce cap for me, but I thought better of it.

From time to time, I zoned out on the proceeding. At one point a vivid picture of Chinese Communist revolutionary justice came into my head. The Shanghai *ayi*, there in her village in rural Jiangxi, one of the poorest provinces, holding forth in a large hut in her capacity of *duizhang* [team head] of her *shengchan dui* [production team], lording it over her comrades, humorlessly brandishing the *Little Red Book* in the face of a cowering revolutionary "criminal", the "masses" competing to garner her favor by insulting and denouncing the accused.

Hours went by. The experience was grueling because it was so boring. I don't know why I let them go on so long. Maybe it was the theatrical aspect, maybe a desire to know where this was going. I started to doze off, only to be brought back to consciousness by the sharp voice of the Shanghai *ayi*. Perhaps the most amazing thing was their ability to ask the same question, to go over the same shallow subject matter so many times. Who knows how long this proceeding could have gone on had she been in her prime, but finally her endurance reached its limit.

Just as the Shanghai *ayi* looked as though she would keel over -- it was lucky that by now the three of us were sitting on the floor -- I got a fresh wind and resolved to get them to relax. The Tibetan breathing techniques! I felt absolutely inspired. I had tried before without success to teach them to Mr. Z. and the Shanghai *ayi*, but now I would demonstrate with an opera DVD. I looked around for one with Maestro Kraus, but sensing the restlessness of the Shanghai *ayi*, I settled upon an equally edifying exemplar, Boris Christoff as Philip II of Spain, glowering on the cover of Verdi's *Don Carlo*. This incomparable Bulgarian bass' performance would demonstrate the all-important high chest position and expansion of the ribs.

I gave the Shanghai *ayi* and "YY" a brief lecture on the opera, but that failed to excite their slightest interest. After a few moments of the overture which likewise did not get them in the mood, I described Christoff's unforgettable Carnegie Hall concert in 1980, at age 66, how Fredric and I had sat high up so that we could experience the mighty voice make the hall ring like a huge bell. I now felt so invigorated that I could have gone on all night. But I noticed a look of disgust mixed with exhaustion on the Shanghai *ayi*'s face. "YY" was almost asleep. Before I could play more than a few bars of King Philip's heart rending aria, "Ella giammai m'amo" ("She never loved me"), the Shanghai *ayi* staggered to her feet, giving "YY" a sharp kick and bringing him to.

Dui niu tan qin [Playing a violin for cows], I thought. Undeterred, I stood up, too, and insisted that first "YY" and then the Shanghai *ayi* place their hands on my back, so that they could feel how I flared out the back ribs and maximized the breathing function without effort, how that also produces relaxation in non-singing mode.

["Do you see what I mean, 'YY'??"] "YY" nodded perfunctorily as he looked nervously at his mother and grunted something in Shanghainese to her.

When it was her turn, the Shanghai *ayi* instead snapped at "YY": *Wenjian* [The document]!

"YY" pulled out a folded sheet of paper from his pocket. The "document" was a single sentence in Chinese, in "YY"'s hand:

["The undersigned, Mr. Rothman, hereby admits that he is guilty of having severe insomnia."]

I could see that further elaborations on breathing technique should be postponed, but I was highly amused at their naïve, faux legalism.

["*Ayi!* 'Admits'? 'Guilty'? Of what? So, insomnia is a crime in China? What's the maximum sentence? Do I need a lawyer?]

["We can't be responsible for your insomnia"], hissed the Shanghai *ayi* as she motioned to "YY" to give me the pen that he was holding.

["Should I write 'insomniac devil' next to my name?"] I asked.

The faces of the Shanghai *ayi* and "YY" showed no more appreciation for this joke than my previous ones. So, I signed, smiling at the Cultural Revolutionary reality show of which I had just been the star. "This is the real thing," I said to myself. "This is living history."

Ah, yinggai gaigezhang! Wo qu na Z. xiansheng suo songgeiwode zhang [Oh, it must be sealed! I'll go get the seal that Mr. Z. gave me].

I applied the seal to the document, but before the ink could dry, the Shanghai *ayi* grabbed the paper out of my hands and motioned abruptly to "YY":

Zoule [We're out of here]!

"YY" dawdled, but after he saw the expression on his mother's face, he scurried after her. Usually so polite to me, they neglected to say goodbye or look back.

The "meeting" left a strange feeling that slowly turned to anger. That nonsensical "confession", what was that all about?

chapter fifteen

The thought of that "meeting" and the sad state of the apartment made me feel dizzy. What was going on? Nothing made sense, no explanation served. I had to lie down. Luckily, the bedroom was relatively untouched. I cleared off the bed, turned on the sound machine, closed the black-out curtain, lay down under one of Beijing *Ayi*'s elegant comforters, wishing very much to be at the China World Apartments under Beijing *Ayi*'s vigilant wing and the protection of an effective security force. Here, I could not even go to the building guards because I knew that the Shanghai *ayi* had befriended them.

I began to breathe gently and evenly through nose and mouth, deeply into the back, allowing the breath to travel up and down the spine, into the head, the neck, the upper back to the lower back, down the legs and into the toes, massaging away with the touch of the breath both physical and psychic pain. As I calmed down, the sweet face of S. *Rinpoche*, beloved master at the Tibetan institute, appeared in my consciousness. The nervous, tingling sensations that had agitated me increasingly since I had gotten back to Shanghai seemed to subside. I was unaware whether I slept or not. Sleeping or daydreaming, other memories, mostly lovely ones, came to mind.

A few nights before the "criticism-education" meeting, at 3am, loud screaming erupted on the street outside the bar in the shopping center below, followed by tearful bawling. A drunken lovers' quarrel. Silence then prevailed. Then, someone started to practice the flute in the old quarter across the alley. "Amazing. 4:30am is the only time this musician has to practice? Why have I never heard this before?" From long experience with neighbors who objected to my singing practice at all hours, I thought, "Surely, this person has the neighbors' consent." Then, a baritone from another corner started to vocalize, then sang something that I didn't recognize. A soprano began to sing. It was impossible to pinpoint the origin of these sounds. "Do these people coordinate their practice? These are real musicians. Is the soprano that sweet lady, the opera singer?"

My mind floated back to a still more magical experience a few days before the dawn concert. The old quarter was not really ancient; almost nothing in Shanghai dates from before the First Opium War (1839-42). But by Shanghai standards, it looked very old, and I loved to wander there and chat up the residents and take photographs. It was a golden October day. I took my camera, went downstairs, walked across the alley, through an open, rusted iron gate, and into another world. Many residents were out and about. The little stalls were filled with fresh vegetables and seafood and household items. Some people recognized me from prior visits, and I recognized some of them. I strolled slowly down the lane, exchanging nods and smiles.

When I took photographs, I did so with a vengeance, an inordinate number of shots, from every conceivable angle. Since many people do not like having a camera pointed at them, not to mention in a society where people have good reason to fear being photographed, I had thought up a gambit. I would ask the adults for permission to photograph the children and sing out praises about how beautiful and intelligent-looking the children were, getting the adults to relax their guard. Then, I could take as many shots as I wanted. One of my favorite subjects was knots of people gambling. There was no need for artifice as to them; they were so wrapped up with their cards and boards that almost nothing would have turned their attention to me.

On that splendid day, I took many photos. As I finished shooting a particularly quaint courtyard and thought about walking home, a well-dressed couple in their early sixties emerged from one of the ramshackle-looking dwellings that formed the courtyard. They had such a pleasant demeanor, and I greeted them cheerfully. They responded with warm smiles and stopped to talk. It turned out that the wife sang Western opera and had studied in Moscow. I was amazed to find such a person there. I told them that I too had sung opera, that my favorite bass was Boris Christoff. The mention of him sent them into raptures. They abandoned whatever they had planned to do and invited me to lunch in their home. After staring for over a year at the old quarter from my study and terrace, which I could see from where we were standing, and wondering what these places looked like inside, now I was to find out. I followed them up a narrow staircase with a combination of light heartedness and sense of achievement.

The apartment was immaculate, tastefully furnished, airy, and surprisingly spacious. It seemed to span the second floors of at least two small houses. An old man was sitting in a chair near a window in the living room, reading a newspaper. He was the father of the husband. The wife pointed to a large, framed poster on the wall with a photograph of a handsome acrobat with a remarkably engaging smile. Then she pointed to the old man who sprang out of his chair and assumed the same attitude and position that he had taken maybe 50 years before for the photograph.

Simple, mostly packaged, Western-style foods were served for lunch. They asked about *Pavaloti* [Pavarotti] whose concert in the Forbidden City they had watched on television. We discussed vocal technique and opera. We talked about Christoff and his great roles in Russian and Italian repertoire. When lunch was finished, the wife, rising with the air of a diva, went to the spinet piano, sang a scale, gave herself a pitch and then sang a Tchaikovsky song *a capella* with a fine soprano voice, beautifully produced, with a distinctly Slavic timbre. I knew the song, and I was genuinely impressed. They asked me to sing something, but I demurred, a little sadly. I hadn't practiced singing since a recital in Beijing in 2002, so I told them that I had a cold and asked her to sing some more. She sang four pieces in all, a wonderful artist. In parting, we agreed that she and I would think about duets to sing together and that they would come to my apartment to watch the DVD with Christoff.

My head was spinning with delight as I returned home. I couldn't believe the confluence of arts and cultures that I had just experienced, the sheer thrill of making such marvelous friends, my delight at getting a glimpse of the domestic world of the old district, and the prospect of having such a lovely soprano with whom to sing.

The Shanghai *ayi* was sitting on the couch in the living room. I started to exclaim about my adventure, but a bitter expression came over her face that stopped me short. She left abruptly, without saying goodbye, without even saying why she had come. "Maybe she's jealous," I thought, for once perhaps insightful into the character of the Shanghai *ayi*.

chapter sixteen

A s I awoke from this dream or reverie, my mind was still focused on the Shanghai *ayi*. Her furtive entrance into the trashed apartment, the lack of surprise on her face at the wild disorder, her refusal to say a single word to me, even to deny that she had done it or look hurt or surprised when I accused her, above all that look of angry contempt on her face. Then, I began to reflect on her untoward behavior in recent weeks:

– that she had asked out of the blue a few days before whether I had medical insurance.

   I never had any reason whatsoever to discuss that subject with her, and she seemed annoyed when I told her that I doubted that I was insured in China.

– that time she had showed up at 3am with her meatball soup:

   ["*Ayi*, even my own mother wouldn't have taken this trouble. You must rest. How on earth did you know that I am awake?"]

   "Amazing how devoted she is," I thought after she left. I had meant to tell her what a strong jolt it gave me. Now, I could not figure out why she did it.

– the business about the rent that was due on October 22 or 23:

> I said: ["Tell the landlord that even though economic conditions are terrible, I will commit to an additional six months. It's an investment for me; meanwhile, pay him for the next three months."]

> Her dismissive air struck me; she should have been glad to know that I planned to stay on, considering that she had no other job:

> ["You won't even need three months,"] she murmured, as if to herself, as if I weren't in the room, in a peculiar, flat tone.

– her abrupt announcement that she did not understand my Mandarin (after more than two and one-half years of conversing with me exclusively in that, the only language in which we both could say much more than "yes" and "no"):

> ["I don't understand your Mandarin. What *gabagabagaba* are you speaking? Your insomnia has addled your brains."] I laughed then, and asked her why so much *piqi* [ill temper] which she also pretended to not understand.

– the time when I opened the door of the study at 7am, after another sleepless night, to find the Shanghai *ayi* planted in a chair that she had placed in the corridor.

> She practically leapt at me: ["What are you doing? How dare you?"]

> ["Do what, *Ayi*?"]

> She never came to work earlier than 8:30 or 9am. What was she doing there then? How long had she been there?

– the even worse fit that she threw—was it the day before or the day after that?—when she screamed at me to eat lunch at 10:30am:

["Get over here! Eat! Now!"]

I hadn't been hungry for weeks, and it was also two hours too early for lunch, but she was upset about something, and I wanted to keep the peace, so I forced myself to swallow a few bites, complimenting her cooking more than eating. Usually glad to accept my praise, she banged a pot hard on the kitchen sink and muttered under her breath in Shanghainese in an angry tone, until finally I heard her slam the front door and leave.

– her comment about the camphorwood screen, just the other day:

["Have you spoken to Little "Q." about the screen?"]

How did she know about that? I had discussed with her the problem that I was having getting the screen shipped home, because of its size and fragility, but not that I had talked about it with "Q." or that his father ran an export business that might be able to ship it for me. Was she a mind reader?

Then, I remembered that I had promised the Shanghai *ayi* that if I gave up the apartment, she could have all of the furniture, the stereo, the running machine, and the office equipment; none of these was damaged.

And that "criticism-education" meeting!

I did not know why the Shanghai *ayi* trashed the apartment, but there seemed little doubt that she had done it. I felt as sadly alone as I had ever felt in my life. I wondered who to turn to. Fredric was beset with his company's problems in the financial crisis. We had a brief and somewhat abrupt call a few nights before; he barely seemed to have time to breathe. What point in worrying him about me; there was no way that he could come to Shanghai.

"Maybe it's the financial crisis," I thought, in reflecting on the fact that not a single one of my Chinese or non-Chinese friends was in Shanghai.

Where the Hell was "U."? After telling me over and over that she would be there months before I arrived, a week after I got there she first emailed to say that she would not be back until October 18, some "family issue", then most recently, not until the 26th. "Damn her. I wouldn't have come back here but for her stupid cooing. 'Dying to see yoooo, miss yoooo soooooo much.' My ass. What a dummy, what the hell am I doing here."

More out of frustration than fear, I decided to change my plane ticket the next day and take the first flight to San Francisco. I got out of bed to look for something but got right back under the covers when I saw the chaos in the rest of the apartment.

chapter seventeen

I wondered whether I could finally fall asleep. I let out a big sigh and
tried to get in touch with my breathing again. In, out, in, out, equally

through nose and mouth, each inhalation and exhalation slower and more gentle and more complete, tip of the tongue resting on the gum line of the upper teeth. "It's really very simple, isn't it," I thought. Slowly, I relaxed, as images of the wonderful experience that I had that very morning came to mind.

The day before, I had emailed to "YY" to tell him that I wanted to take up Mr. Z. on his longstanding invitation to accompany him on his daily walk at dawn in the park. After yet another sleepless night, when 6am arrived, I called the Shanghai *ayi*'s apartment. I had not hesitated to call so early, because they always told me that they were awake by then, she to go out to buy food, and Mr. Z. for his walk. Mr. Z. answered the phone and gladly agreed to meet at the corner of the park nearest my building.

["You see, Mr. Rothman, you should always come out at this hour. Can you smell the oxygen in the air? I told you, it is at its maximum now."]

["Yes, Mr. Z., the air is amazingly fresh."]

And so it was, that glorious morning.

The park filled up rapidly. Some people exercised in groups, there were grannies in drum and cymbal corps, most did his or her own thing, kicking the legs up onto a bar, stretching, hip rolls, knee rolls, breathing exercises, sword practice, fan dances, *tai qi*.

Songbirds sang their hearts out in cages hung everywhere in the branches of the still-flowering bushes and trees.

["Mr. Rothman, you see, even the birds are happy for all the oxygen that they are getting"]

So they were, and they sang a gorgeous symphony.

Everyone in the park seemed to know Mr. Z. He exchanged greetings with dozens of people.

Xianzai daole "silingbu" [Now we have arrived at "military field head-quarters"], Mr. Z. announced as we reached the top of a leafy knoll where there was a large *ting* [pavilion] crammed full with more than 20 elderly people who were conversing animatedly. The youngest was 76, a woman doctor who wheeled herself over to the center of the group when we arrived, and the oldest a man of 93. Mr. Z. was a mere child by comparison, but they all greeted him with genuine respect.

Zhewei shi Luo Lüshi, ta shi guoji lüshi. Ta jiang Putonghua [This is Lawyer Rothman, he is an international lawyer. He speaks Mandarin], Mr. Z. introduced me, with emphasis on the *guoji* [international].

Expressions of warm welcome rang out. Everyone exchanged jokes for about 45 minutes. I came out with my cleverest idioms and wordplay, and created new ones on the spot, just as they did. The crowd roared with laughter and approval as one chimed in after another. Their ancient faces were so wonderfully kind, their eyes so alight with joy, that had I been in the US I would have kissed each one of them. Instead, I shook hands with them, one by one, folding both of mine around both of theirs. Mr. Z. beamed with pride.

As we took leave of the group, I said to Mr. Z.: ["I am really honored that you would introduce me to these venerable friends. Quite obviously, they all admire your learning very much."]

Nali, nali [Not at all, not at all], Mr. Z. replied.

We agreed to walk in the park together often and to visit again with those delightful people in the *ting*.

As I lay in bed, savoring that matchless experience, I thought, "How could I have had such a morning to come back to this? From apex to nadir, all within a few hours." I sat up and laughed out loud for the bitter irony of it.

I dismissed any idea that Mr. Z. was involved in the attack on the apartment. But my heart ached for the inevitable rupture that I foresaw. I wracked my brain to find some reason for the Shanghai *ayi*'s actions. Could one of them be terribly ill? "No. Mr. Z. never would have been so carefree this morning. He always tells me, even when he is sick."

Sometime after midnight, a tremendous ruckus broke out in the hall outside the apartment. Was it some drunks from the bar downstairs? "I hope they don't live here," I thought. I got up and looked through the peephole in the front door. The view was blocked, but there was much pounding on the door and stomping of feet.

Opening the door, I was face to face with a gang of thugs, tall, short, pudgy, thin, 10-12 in number. They greeted me with angry expressions and gestures and shouts in Shanghainese that I did not understand except that they were the opposite of friendly greetings. Some wore guard or police or fireman uniforms with insignia, some wore uniforms with no insignia, some were in street clothing, most were smoking cigarettes.

As I stepped into the hall, they contracted into one unbroken stack of people that melted back to the stairwell and down the stairs. The human and tobacco stench almost knocked me over. I felt a surge of that odd electric current, a sort of buzz, not pleasant, not unpleasant. As calmly as I could, I went up to the pudgy one in front:

Shenma yisi, gan shenma [What's the meaning, what are you up to]?

He said nothing, but I could smell his disgusting breath which reeked of cheap *baijiu* [white spirits]. The doors of the neighboring apartments opened, a few heads stuck out, then jerked back in, the doors slammed shut. The mob made guttural, unintelligible sounds that gradually diminished to a murmur. I looked them over again, and this time in a ferocious voice demanded:

Shenma yisi, you shenma shi? [What's the meaning, what business have you]?

For a split second, they seemed bewitched, in a trance. Then, the one in front shook his fist at me and the others followed suit. Raising my chest as if I were doing an impression of Mussolini, I bellied up to the one in front and said in a deliberately understated tone:

Cao ni, cao ni made sha bi [Go fuck yourself, fuck your mother's stupid cunt].

Once again, the thugs stopped in mid-motion, as if in a *tableau vivant*. For a few seconds, they showed no sign of leaving, of lowering their fists, or of moving at all, then suddenly the mass of people stirred and slowly started toward me, in a single wave. I jumped back inside the apartment and slammed the door in their faces. I heard the neighbors' doors open and shut again and watched through the peephole as the thugs milled about, banged on my door, muttered and gesticulated to each other. After twenty minutes, they trooped into the stairwell and downstairs, enveloped in a dense cloud of cigarette smoke.

I caught sight of the Mao-Lin Biao placard. I never would be able to carry it in my luggage if I had to run out of there, so I knocked a piece off the top with a hammer, so that no one would get an unblemished gift of it, and made black "Xs" with a marker pen over the image of Lin Biao, for political correctness. Looking around again, I spotted my Yale directory. I checked to see that the coast was clear and placed the directory and the placard at right angles in the corner to the left outside the front door.

Most people would understand why I thought to use the placard as a protective totem. Why the Yale directory? Because I thought that Yale's clout and renown might be intimidating. That of course assumed that at least one of the thugs could recognize "Yale" and read the thing. But I also wanted to reassure my neighbors in the apartment to the right, who did read English and with whom I used to chat in passing, that I wasn't the type to consort with the low-lives who had created the disturbance that night, and I put Post-its next to the names of George W. Bush, George H.W. Bush, Dick Cheney, Bill Clinton, Hillary Clinton, and Clark Randt, the US ambassador.

Contemptuous of the thugs, I left the front door completely open. Whether or not the totems had any effect, no one bothered me again that night. I spent the hours until dawn in the study, far away down a hall out of sight of the front door, typing and reading emails, surfing the Internet, not once going back to see whether the thugs returned.

At daybreak, I finally thought to check. The placard and the directory had not been disturbed. I took them inside, closed the door, lay down on the bed without the slightest hope of falling asleep. Part of me realized that nothing in my life ever would be the same. Yet, now that the thugs had left and not come back for all those hours with my door ajar, I also entertained the notion that the immediate trouble was past, wherever it had come from, forgetting that I had held that same thought after the confrontation with the Shanghai *ayi*, only hours before the thugs showed up.

Thus, I tricked myself into believing that I had seized control of the situation, whereas nothing could have been further from the truth. I did not even know what the "situation" was. I should have realized that what had gone on in the apartment could not possibly be tied off and concluded because I wanted it to be so, not in any country, certainly not in China. It should have been clear that there was much more behind these events than a mere housekeeper's anger or her personal problems, that these could not have been random occurrences.

Maybe it was that *laowai* invulnerability illusion, and all those exotic travels. Maybe it was a sort of mental armor that I adopted after an attack on me Junior Year that left my jaw shattered. I was terrified of violence but more terrified at the thought of being a coward. I refused to run from bullies, not the townies in New Haven and not these thugs. Maybe it also was a lack of judgment brought on by extreme fatigue, maybe that strange electric current that I had been feeling. But never in my life had I behaved as just now, and nothing surprised me more than that.

Whatever motivated my decisions, most sensible people would not have gone as far as I did in standing my ground. However, the facts that later became known might lead one to the conclusion that, at some point well before October 21, 2008, I no longer had viable options at all and in fact that by staying put, I might have given myself a better chance of surviving. It would be difficult to say. As I contemplated that dreary morning of October 22, I said out loud: "The Hell with those thugs and that bitch of an *ayi*. No one is running me out of here."

But my ordeal was far from over, rather it had just begun.

epilogue

The November 2011 murder of British businessman Neil Heywood at a mangy Chongqing hotel by Gu Kailai, the wife of Bo Xilai, the party secretary of Chongqing, burst into the news in February 2012, at that most delicate of times, in the midst of the decennial Chinese Communist leadership transition, from the "Fourth Generation" led by Hu Jintao to the "Fifth Generation" to be led by Xi Jinping.[10] With the formal succession to take place in Fall 2012, the revelation of the murder precipitated a succession crisis more complex and consequential than any since October 1976, one month after Mao's death, when Hua Guofeng, at the instigation of Party elders led by Marshal Ye Jianying, arrested Jiang Qing and the rest of the Gang of Four, thus ending formally the Cultural Revolution.

At the beginning of February 2012, Bo Xilai was China's political rock star. Seemingly destined for greatness, he was youthful, charismatic, and media savvy. As the boss of Chongqing, a huge city-province that had been carved out of Sichuan Province and given the same rank as Beijing, Shanghai, and Tianjin as a "directly-ruled city", he was in charge of top priority mega-infrastructure projects which were the focal point of a gigantic effort to bring the much less developed central and western regions of the country closer to the level of the rapidly developing coastal regions.

---

10 The "Third Generation" was led by Jiang Zemin and the "Second Generation" by Deng Xiaoping. The "First Generation" was that of Mao Zedong and Liu Shaoqi.

Considered a shoo-in for a place in the topmost tier of the Chinese leadership, the all-powerful Standing Committee of the Politburo of the Communist Party, Bo Xilai was popular for the tremendous amount of public and private money that went to Chongqing during his tenure, for his brutal crackdown on organized crime,[11] and for his "Sing Red" campaigns that featured Maoist slogans and mass performances of revolutionary songs. Bo was a *taizi* [princeling], a member of the Communist royalty who owed positions and wealth to their being the offspring or married to the offspring of top leaders. Bo Xilai was the son of a leading revolutionary general, Bo Yibo, one of the "Eight Immortals,"[12] and he had serious support in the People's Liberation Army (PLA).

Zhou Yongkang was Bo Xilai's immediate protector. In early 2012, Zhou was the Minister of Public Security and one of nine members of the Standing Committee, in command of a huge internal security portfolio that encompassed courts, procuratorate, prisons, Internet surveillance, and millions of secret police and paramilitary forces. His budget was said to exceed the one for national defense. Zhou's influence also reached deep into the Chinese petroleum industry and Sichuan Province both of which he had run before his elevation to the Ministry and the Standing Committee.

The *kaoshan* [reliable mountain, or godfather] of both Bo and Zhou was none other than Jiang Zemin the most senior of all Party Elders. It was Jiang to whom Deng Xiaoping turned in 1989 to lead the Party when the nationwide Tiananmen Square-inspired demonstrations spun out of control, the Party's most desperate hour since Liberation.

So far as can be determined, Gu Kailai, killed Neil Heywood because he had demanded a bigger cut of the huge sums that he was allegedly

---

11 Much of the crackdown was shown later to be as criminal in method and intent as the guilty among the targeted people and organizations, some of the targets being completely innocent.

12 They were Deng Xiaoping and seven other top revolutionary leaders who survived Mao's decades of political purges and regained senior posts or political clout after the arrest of the Gang of Four.

laundering for Bo Xilai's family. Gu first turned to Wang Lijun, Bo's hand-picked police chief, to plan a fake drug sting in which Heywood was to be shot dead. When Wang backed out, Gu lured Heywood to the Lucky Holiday Hotel, where she murdered Heywood herself by drizzling cyanide down his throat as her assistant held him down on a bed. Wang helped her cover up the murder, complete with a cremation with no autopsy. The British government played along and accepted the story that Heywood, a known tee-totaler, died from massive alcohol consumption. Two officers of the British Consulate in Chongqing actually attended the cremation.

Nothing would have been known of Heywood's fate, or the corruption involving Bo Xilai's family, but for the fact that investigators were closing in on Wang Lijun for corruption in a prior post. Seeking Bo's protection, Wang confronted Bo with the details of Heywood's murder. Instead of protection, Bo gave him a punch in the face and a demotion. Bo began arresting Wang's allies and circulated on the Internet forged mental health records that purported to show that Wang suffered from depression. Wang must have realized that he was about to be murdered himself, with a staged suicide as the cover up, a common scenario in China. On February 6, 2012, he raced hundreds of miles west of Chongqing to the US Consulate in Chengdu and told the Consulate officers about Heywood's murder and other damaging information about Bo and Gu.

There are many critical turning points in this unparalleled political drama, but one is that punch in the face that Bo delivered to Wang Lijun. Had Wang not been motivated to flee to Chengdu, or had he been minutes later getting to the US Consulate, Bo's henchmen, hot on his heels, would have grabbed him, the whole story would have been suppressed, and Bo and above all Bo's protectors and allies, would have retained considerable leverage. With the stories about Bo and his wife not just public, but made public in a deeply humiliating way for China, Wang returned, or was returned, to the custody of agents rushed to Chengdu from Beijing, on the promise that he would be given "vacation-style hospital treatment."[13]

Bo Xilai's business associates and Wang Lijun's underlings in the Chongqing police department were hauled in first and dealt with briskly and secretly, except for the sentences. In May 2012, Bo was placed under *shuanggui*, the Party's infamous, secret internal investigation process, for corruption and for abuse of power concerning the Neil Heywood murder.

The next step was Gu Kailai's trial, in August 2012, for Heywood's murder, then Wang Lijun's the following month, for his role in covering it up. Both proceedings, held in remote cities, were the very definition of Communist show trials, except some 21st Century-style, tear jerker moments in Gu's trial.[14]

With the trial of Bo Xilai in August 2013, the real stakes in the Neil Heywood murder were in play.[15] No top level official since Jiang Qing had been put on public trial in what passed for a court or had his or her life put on display in such lurid detail. Nor, in acting publicly against someone of Bo's rank and power, had any leader taken the risks that Xi Jinping has taken since the arrest of Jiang Qing.

---

13 Incredibly, a second major scandal involving the top leadership soon occurred. In March 2012, Ling Gu, the son of Hu Jintao's chief of staff, Ling Jihua, crashed his Ferrari in Beijing while driving mostly naked, in the company of two similarly attired young woman, one ethnic Uighur, the other ethnic Tibetan, leaving Ling Gu and one of the women dead, the other severely injured. This combined an example of gross extravagance and criminally reckless behavior by a son of a top official with a second matter of utmost sensitivity, ethnic minority relations, and thus seriously undermined Hu's power base. Zhou Yongkang is alleged to have arranged payoff money for the families of the two women.

14 The British never challenged the official Chinese accounts, never demanded access to witnesses or evidence, of which nothing was made public except nonsensical fabrications and defamations of Heywood which were introduced as supposed extenuating circumstances. The British attended the Gu and Wang trials without protest and even endorsed them as valid trials.

15 The British did not bother to attend Bo Xilai's trial even though Bo's cover-up of the Heywood murder was central to the case against him.

Bo's trial had its share of drama when he spoke in his defense and vigorously denied the charges, but the political struggle always was implicit, never explicit. Bo had himself and his family members and retainers to worry about, and he was too ambitious not to have entertained the idea of a comeback. He did not dare to adopt Jiang Qing's vituperative tone, much less attack the legitimacy of his accusers and judges as she did hers, at least not in the portions of the trial made public.

Bo got life imprisonment, Gu a suspended death sentence, and Wang a relatively light jail term. Xi has better use for them than to turn them into ashes. In fact, all three are sitting in comfortable cells, and they may well figure in the trial of Zhou Yongkang who is the biggest "tiger" yet snared by Xi.

Zhou's fall required a bit more time to bring about. He made a huge mistake by stating publicly his continued support for Bo when Bo was detained in May 2012. Soon, Zhou was forced into retirement, and he gradually disappeared from sight. All of Zhou's known relatives (other than his son's mother-in-law who lives in the US) were rounded up along with scores of Zhou's and his son's associates. In March 2014, Chinese state media announced that Zhou and the people around him had been detained for investigation for corruption totaling USD $14.5 billion, and in December 2014 that he had been expelled from the Party and that he would stand trial. Zhou's trial should have the greatest potential for fireworks, because his control of internal security must have given him the goods on everyone else in the elite ranks. But Xi may well have outflanked him as he did Bo Xilai, by arresting so many people close to him. And any real fireworks likely will not be out in public. In any case, Zhou's conviction is a foregone conclusion.

Weiji [crisis]. *Wei* means danger. *Ji* means opportunity. The very definition of crisis in Chinese is a situation that combines the two. From the first moments of the succession crisis, Xi Jinping grasped opportunity and embraced rather than fled danger. He managed to control the situation with total aplomb, to make each step appear inevitable, and to use the crisis to become leader-in-fact as opposed to leader-in-waiting. Then, once he formally assumed the top leadership in November 2012, the Neil Heywood murder case became the focal point of Xi's sweeping political purge carried out in the name of fighting corruption which is the basis on which Xi has become the undisputed, supreme leader of China. But until the Heywood murder, the obstacles to any such ascendancy of Xi would have seemed insurmountable.

Xi, a princeling like Bo[16], originally was expected to be first among equals with the other Standing Committee members, like his predecessors, Jiang Zemin and Hu Jintao, and always subject to the unwritten veto power of Party Elders, in accordance with Deng's governance plan that sought to prevent the rise of another all-powerful leader such as Mao. The fact that, unlike Jiang and Hu, Xi was not chosen by Communist Party founders should have further limited his power, not to mention that Bo and Zhou had Jiang in their corner, along with their huge civilian power bases and support in the military and paramilitary. Indeed, rumors circulated of plots and military coups by their supporters as Xi closed the net around Bo.

None of this seems to have intimidated Xi. And if it wasn't clear before the November 2012 Party congress that Xi had become the supreme leader of China, it certainly became clear soon thereafter, as Xi quickly and decisively arrogated power to himself to an extent never before seen

---

16 Xi's father also was a revolutionary general who was purged by Mao and who became a high-level official under Deng Xiaoping, although Xi's father was not one of the "Eight Immortals."

in the 65 years of communist rule, except when Mao was at the zenith of his power.[17]

Xi also has shifted decisively prevailing Party ideology and far outdone Bo Xilai in promoting a neo-Maoist revival in which Communist ideology has been reemphasized along with official self-criticism campaigns, intense emphasis on ideological purity, and purges of any trace of democratic thought in the Party, in the universities, and in the media, especially the Internet. Xi has created an extensive personality cult for himself, brutally repressed human rights advocates, severely narrowed the small scope for individual freedom that had been developing, and made it abundantly clear that by Rule of Law he really has in mind *rule by means of law*. In foreign affairs, Xi has appealed to Chinese nationalism by aggressively, at times belligerently, promoting China's interests in every part of the globe, shedding once and for all Deng's pretense that China is a retiring international presence.

By leading to the downfall of Bo Xilai and Zhou Yongkang, the murder of Neil Heywood played a decisive role in Xi Jinping's extraordinary rise. The sordid revelations that came out as a result of the murder were traumatic and severely damaging to the Party Elders and factions who supported Bo and Zhou and left them defenseless and vulnerable. Very likely, other factors were significant[18], but it is clear that without the leverage provided by the murder, Xi could not have created his virtual monopoly

---

17 Most importantly, the Standing Committee was reduced from nine to seven members which greatly helped Xi concentrate power in his hands. And he became the Chairman of the Party's Central Military Commission (CMC), the effective commander-in-chief of the People's Liberation Army, the single most powerful position in China, simultaneously with his becoming General Secretary in November 2012. Instead of making Xi wait until November 2014, based on the precedent of the Jiang Zemin-Hu Jintao transition, when Jiang kept the CMC chairmanship for the first two years of Hu's term as General Secretary, Hu relinquished the CMC chairmanship in November 2012, possibly because of the Ling Jihua scandal. As a result, Xi has been able to purge the top ranks of the PLA at the same time that he has been purging the Party, the government, and state-owned enterprises. Xi has also placed himself in direct charge of all major governmental areas as chairman of "leading groups" directing everything from the economy to national security.
18 Such as the fall of Ling Jihua.

of political power. Thus, it can be said that neither in life nor in death has a single *laowai* so directly influenced the course of Chinese Communist history as much as Neil Heywood.

Warren Henry Rothman
May 7, 2015

Thank you for your interest in **KAFKA IN CHINA, Part One.** *For updates on the publication of* **Part Two,** *please sign up at: kafkainchina. com/updates. Kindly leave your review of Part One on Amazon, http:// tinyurl.com/nr2bsrj (for the physical book) or on Kindle.*